Mel Bay Presents

A Concise
History
of the *Electric Guitar*

by Adrian Ingram

Visit us on the Web at www.melbay.com — E-mail us at email@melbay.com

Adrian Ingram, one of the foremost authorities on the jazz guitar, has written extensively on the history, players, styles and instruments of the genre. As an educator he ran the prestigious jazz guitar course at Leeds College of Music, England, for almost fifteen years, during which time he was elected a Fellow of the Royal Society of Arts (FRSA) for his outstanding contribution to music education. He holds Masters degrees in music education and music performance as well as classic guitar Fellowships of London conservatories. Adrian Ingram, an internationally acclaimed jazz guitarist, performs at the major festivals and has recorded a number of CDs and several instructional videos.

CONTENTS

3

LIST OF ILLUSTRATIONS

FOREWORD

This book, intended for the general public, music students, and, of course, all guitar players, charts the exciting history of the electric guitar from the early decades of the 20th century up to the present day.

Adrian Ingram, a colleague and friend of mine for many years, has chosen in this concise but thorough history to cover the gamut of styles and personalities whose impact shaped the destiny of the guitar and made such a varied and versatile instrument the predominant factor in so much popular music.

This is undoubtedly one of the first books of its kind to be written by an outstanding performer on the guitar, and so the author has been able to combine insight, scholarly research and an intimate knowledge of the music business with a unique awareness of the history of the instrument, pickups, amplifiers and technical innovations of all kinds. What Adrian Ingram has achieved is not only a concise history of the electric guitar, but also a clear statement of trends and developments of some of the most significant popular music of recent decades.

Whoever studies this book closely will therefore gain a clearer understanding of the guitar's history in all its stylistic variety and, at the same time, become better informed about the complex shifts and patterns of a large slice of contemporary culture.

We would like to express our heartfelt gratitude to William Bay and all his staff at Mel Bay Publications Inc. for making this book and this series possible. We must also thank June Ingram and Elizabeth Wade for their invaluable editorial assistance and support during the preparation of this work.

Graham Wade
General Editor, *ALL ABOUT MUSIC SERIES*

PART I: ANTECEDENTS

1. The Gibson ES150, Pickups and Amplification

The roots of the electric guitar evolved both from the 1930s lap steel Rickenbackers and Gibson's first production line electric archtop: the 1936 ES150. (Gibson always used the letters E.S. for the 'Electric Spanish' series.)

A 1936 ES150 'Charlie Christian' guitar and matching amplifier

Rickenbacker, and their competitors Dobro and National, manufactured lap steels, which were essentially square necked Hawaiian guitars, played not with the fingers of the left hand, but with a metal bar or slide. These diminutive instruments, which rested on the player's lap, were the first to be successfully amplified and, as such, found their way onto numerous recordings, radio broadcasts and even film sets. Their construction, from a solid plank of wood or several smaller pieces laminated together, provided the model for later experiments by Paul Bigsby, Les Paul and Leo Fender, who collectively, yet independently, pioneered the solid-body electric guitar.

The Gibson ES150, on the other hand, was mainly a regular production line archtop, equipped with an early design magnetic pickup. As a mid to low range model, the acoustic Gibson 150 could be amplified relatively easily and cheaply, with no significant change in construction. Because this did not necessitate any retooling, or additional manpower, Gibson was able to enter the electric guitar market rather cautiously, allowing the company to monitor and determine its commitment on the strength of the ES150's success. Whereas Rickenbacker lap steels can be viewed as the precursors to the solid-bodied guitar, the Gibson ES150 was unquestionably the predecessor of a long line of acoustic electrics.

If these two companies produced the antecedents of today's electric guitars, the story of how they developed the means to amplify their instruments is not quite as clear cut. During the 1920s and 30s, several charismatic inventors and tinkerers were working along similar lines; their experiments with amplification fell into two distinct camps: Electrostatic or Electromagnetic.

The earliest known experiments (other than those using phonographs and telephones) were the electrostatic pickups. These were electric devices which transmitted the guitar's vibrations from the body rather than from directly above, or below, the strings. Lloyd Loar, a leading designer at Gibson during the early 1920s, was a strong advocate of this system and together with his colleague L.A. Williams, produced several prototype electric guitars. Using a regular L4 round-hole, acoustic guitar as their test piece, Williams and Loar glued an electrostatic pickup to the underside of the guitar's table (top). The electric cable and connecting socket passed directly through the tailpiece, which was situated in the bottom rim.

There were a number of problems inherent in the design of these pickups. Its high impedance proved problematic, as did its sensitivity to humidity. Furthermore it would only work with a short connecting cable, which severely limited its professional use. However, its main strength, the fact that the electrostatic unit was able to amplify both nylon/gut and steel strings, would not be realized and fully developed until the 1960s.

While the early electrostatic pickup was rather crude, and susceptible to interference, crackles and hum, it did, nevertheless, provide the catalyst for further experimentation, not only by Gibson, but also the company's rivals such as Dobro, Epiphone, Harmony and Rickenbacker. Paradoxically, whilst the concept of amplifying stringed instruments had become firmly established during the late 1920s, the underlying principle upon which it was originally based was discarded or, at least, shelved until the advent of 'solid-state' transistor technology in the 1960s.

The future lay, not as Williams and Loar had assumed, in transmitting the instrument's vibrations via the body, but rather through the development of an electro-magnet, which, when placed directly above or below the strings, would further amplify their vibrations. These vibrations were picked up and converted into an electrical signal which was, in turn, amplified, hence the generic term 'pickup' for all types of electro magnetic attachments. Of course, this new type of pickup necessitated steel strings and, from the outset, all commercially manufactured amplified stringed instruments were fitted with them. The majority of stringed instruments which used either gut, or a combination of gut and metal strings such as the guitar, mandolin, banjo, ukulele and lap steel guitar could be readily converted. Some, however, and in particular, the more delicate classic guitar, which depended

9

upon gut strings for its tone, (not to mention its structural stability) could not be so readily converted and have, therefore, never been closely associated with the trappings of amplification.

For this reason, the antecedents of the electric guitar, and the parameters of its definition, can be traced back to the appearance of the electro magnetic pickups. The principal pioneers of this pickup were George Beauchamp and Paul Barth. They suspected that if radio waves could be amplified, then so too could vibration waves. Beauchamp's son, Nolan, related the following story to *Guitar Player* in 1974:

> My uncle had a Brunswick phonograph, and my father took the pickup out, extended the wires, and mounted it on a [block of wood] two-by-four with a single string. That's how he first proved that his theory was practical. He then began perfecting his six-string pickup.

2. Beauchamp, Barth and Rickenbacker

This was around 1930. By 1931 a prototype electric 'lap steel' guitar was produced. As an experimental model Beauchamp and Barth, together with Adolph Rickenbacker and Harry Watson (another National employee), were unconcerned with aesthetics.

The crude hand-made instrument, with its small round body and long neck, was originally named the 'Fry Pan', but electric guitar historians and collectors have since corrupted this to the 'Frying Pan'.

In 1932, Beauchamp and Barth moved on from National to form their own company in conjunction with Adolph Rickenbacker. The new company adopted the curious name of Ro-Pat-In and began manufacturing aluminium versions of the Fry Pan lap steel. These lap steels, with their 'horseshoe' style magnetic pickups, were ostensibly the first electric string instruments to be mass-produced; and while, by modern day standards, the numbers manufactured were relatively small, they nevertheless paved the way for later developments.

Beauchamp had filed patents, with the US Patent Office, in 1933 and 1934, but these were not officially granted until 1937, despite the fact that the Patent Office had legally assigned the rights of Ro-Pat-In company in 1935. This patent, however, was for a specific type of magnetic pickup, which featured a large horseshoe shaped magnet, extending both below and above the strings. Although it was a cumbersome affair, the horseshoe unit was quickly adopted by other guitar manufacturers, notably Dobro, Vega, National and Epiphone. By 1934, the Ro-Pat-In company became the 'Electro String Instrument Corporation' under which banner it manufactured both Electro and Rickenbacker lap steels.

There was fierce rivalry between this new company and Dobro, not least because some members of staff had worked, at various times, for both companies.

Ironically, Dobro made a handful of electrified 'resonator' guitars as early as 1933/4, where the internal resonating device was replaced by a horseshoe magnet pickup.

Conversely, Rickenbacker's guitar shaped version of the Fry Pan lap steel, was launched around 1935, some examples of which were made with a round, as opposed to square, neck. These so-called Style B models were mainly marketed as square necked lap steel guitars, although a small but significant number of 'Spanish' guitar models were made. Effectively this small run of Style B Rickenbacker Spanish guitars proved to be not only the first electric guitars, but also the first solid-bodied 'Spanish' guitars to be manufactured in appreciable numbers.

11

The B Style's diminutive size and short 22¾" scale fingerboard marks the instrument as something of a novelty today, and its sound and performance would certainly not compare with modern-day electric guitars. In many respects, the late 1930s Slingerland, style 401, electric 'Spanish' guitar was, with its more usable 25" fingerboard scale length and larger body, much closer in spirit and design to the contemporary solid-bodied electric guitar.

Despite the pioneering work of visionaries like Loar, Beauchamp and Barth, the electric guitar, as we know it today, was designed and refined during the later 40s and early 50s. Of course, the embryonic developments are both interesting and significant, but it was not until the appearance of Fender's Telecaster and Stratocaster, together with the Gibson Les Paul, that the electric guitar became a vital entity in its own right.

How we arrived at this point is important, but the electric guitar's 'glory years' closely correspond with the emergence of rock'n' roll. Indeed, it has since become the very personification of the music. Yet, one of the instrument's greatest strengths lies in its versatility and ability to function as an essential tool in a variety of musical genres.

PART II: PIONEERS

3. Pioneers and Early Performers

While it is possible to identify and catalog early manufacturers of embryonic forms of the electric guitar, it is much more difficult to document the chronology of the earliest performers, especially when several players have emphatically staked their claim to being the first electric guitarist.

Although most of their 'pioneer' stories are completely plausible, in truth, we will probably never know who the first electric guitarist really was. Indeed, it is likely that there was essentially no 'first' electric guitarist per se, but rather several, working contemporaneously in different geographical areas. These guitarists would probably also have played in various musical styles too, ranging from blues and jazz to popular dance music and western swing.

It would appear that the common link between all early electric guitarists was a preoccupation with the emulation of horn players (horn being the generic term for the saxophone and trumpet). Big bands were fashionable, as were smaller swing combos; both featured saxophones and trumpets in their front-line, instruments which were among the loudest and therefore most easily heard.

Guitarists, it seems, lusted for a similar position in the spotlight, and were reported to be rather discontented with their perceived function as rhythmic time keepers! Their role of four-to-the-bar chuggers, in the supportive rhythm section had, of course, been inherited from the banjo players who preceded them. Furthermore, the guitar's diminutive voice and lack of cutting power rendered it unsuitable for single-note solos especially when played in ensemble together with brass and reed.

13

The guitar duos of Eddie Lang (1902-1933) and Lonnie Johnson (1894-1970), Dick McDonough (1904-1938) and Carl Kress (1907-1965), and a few brave attempts in bigger bands by players such as Alan Reuss (1915-1988) and Teddy Bunn (1909-1978), demonstrated that the guitar was technically as capable of soloing as the horns, hampered only by its inherently weak tone and lack of volume.

Early pioneers of the electric guitar saw amplification as the vehicle which would enable them to compete with the horns. It was a liberator, a tool which would allow them not only to join the horn section in tutti ensemble passages, but also to become soloists on equal terms with the featured saxophonists and trumpeters. It is hardly surprising, therefore, that with few exceptions almost all of the early electric guitarists have cited either saxophonists or trumpeters as their major influences.

4. Charlie Christian

This desire, to be taken on the same footing as other front-line band instrumentalists, led to Charlie Christian's memorable article in *Downbeat* (December 1, 1939), the headline to which asserted: 'Guitarmen, Wake Up and Pluck! Wire for Sounds; Let 'Em Hear You Play.' In the same article, Christian went on to provide an overview of the electric guitar and its major exponents in the jazz field, many of whom actually predated Christian in their use of the instrument.

There can be no dispute, however, that Charlie Christian's strident horn-like style and commercial exposure, with the Benny Goodman Band, was a catalyst for the increasing appearance of the electric guitar in a cross-section of musical styles. It would be no exaggeration, therefore, to suggest that the handful of recordings by Christian, made between 1939 and 1941, irrevocably changed the face of popular music.

On hearing these recordings, Eldon Shamblin, Junior Barnard, Jimmy Wyble and Cameron Hill introduced the electric guitar to Country and Western audiences during the early 40s. For the same reason Les Paul (with Bing Crosby) and Oscar Moore (with Nat King Cole) could be heard regularly on radio and recordings playing the swing-based popular music of the day. Christian also motivated an entire generation of jazz guitarists who emerged throughout the 40s, the most significant being Irving Ashby, Barney Kessel, Chuck Wayne, Mary Osborne, Jimmy Raney and Tal Farlow.

Charlie Christian on the cover of Guitar Player, March 1982

Despite the enormity of his impact, Charlie Christian led a tragically short life, about which surprisingly little is known. Born in Dallas (1919), he grew up in Oklahoma and paid his dues in a variety of Kansas City style jazz bands. These blues-based units provided the music for dances, and were required to place strong emphasis upon a strict four beats to the measure rhythm.

15

The Kansas City Style made much use of riffs, which were essentially short rhythmic phrases repeated at set places in the music and often sequenced through the entire chord progression. Saxophonists, in particular, were heavily featured, with their penchant for long fluid lines, shifting accents and a liberal helping of notes per measure. Ben Webster, Herschel Evans, Lester Young and Buster Smith were among the saxophonists with whose music Christian would have been familiar. Indeed, jazz historians have long drawn close parallels between the improvisations of Lester Young and Charlie Christian, both of whom are considered to be important jazz innovators.

Christian's early years were spent playing both the double bass and acoustic guitar. He turned to the electric guitar in 1937, and played it so well that he soon became a local celebrity. As his reputation spread, other guitarists came to hear him, including such future greats as T-Bone Walker (an early friend) and Barney Kessel.

It was inevitable that a player of Christian's talent and reputation would soon move on to greater things. When jazz entrepreneur John Hammond arranged for him to fly to Los Angeles to cut a record with Benny Goodman, he was ready. While the initial meeting did not go too well, or result in any recordings, Goodman's early scepticism was quickly dispelled and their first recording together, *Flying Home*, became a huge success.

Christian went on to record more sides with Benny Goodman, both with the full band and sextet. By 1940, he was also regularly jamming into the early hours at Minton's Playhouse, a basement room in the Hotel Cecil, Harlem. Minton's was a nightclub managed by Christian's long-standing friend, the bandleader/saxophonist Teddy Hill. It became affectionately known as 'Teddy's Place', a magnet for musicians, both the young innovators like pianist Thelonious Monk, drummer Kenny Clarke and trumpeter Dizzy Gillespie, and for those impressionable young players seeking inspiration and direction. Christian played there whenever possible, and, along with the aforementioned musicians, became a prime mover in the development of the bebop jazz style.

Fortunately, many of the late-night sessions were recorded and released to the public (*The Harlem Jazz Scene* - 1941, Esoteric Records ES 548). While these important recordings did not reach as wide an audience as the more commercially biased Goodman sides, the urgency and raw energy which characterize the 'live' sessions greatly influenced the future direction of small group jazz and, in particular, the electric guitar. Christian's fondness for rhythmic displacement of the basic beat, for example, provided the model for many of the stylistic developments which were to follow.

Guitaristically, Charlie Christian was primarily a Gibson man with a particular fondness for the Gibson ES150 and ES250. The ES (Electric Spanish) 150 was the company's first production-line electric guitar introduced in 1936. Rather than being a fully committed entry into the amplified guitar arena, the ES150 was essentially the company's existing L50 acoustic archtop, with the addition of a bar (blade) magnet pickup.

Unlike the horseshoe pickup, earlier developed by Rickenbacker and fitted to the electric guitars made by Harmony, Vega, National, Rickenbacker and Epiphone, the two heavy magnets of Gibson's bar pickup were suspended, directly beneath the carved spruce tops of both the ES150 and ES250 models.

Only the coil-bobbin, which surrounded the metal blade and three height/angle adjusting screws were visible. The bobbin was covered and protected by a black plastic plate, which had a single white decorative binding. A finer, alternating, double white/black binding was used on the pickups for the 1938-1940 ES150 and 1939-1941 ES250.

All versions of these bar magnets had a single metal blade, which protruded through the centre of the bobbin, a feature which resulted in the term bar, or blade, pickup. Because Christian was so closely identified with these early Gibson electric guitars, the pickups became known as Charlie Christian bar pickups.

Although only available for a short period in 1938-1940, the larger and more ornate ES250 Charlie Christian guitar was produced in far smaller numbers and with less consistency of features and fittings.

Apart from its 17" (as opposed to 16") width body, optional blonde finish and deluxe ornamentation, the principal feature which separated the ES150 from the ES250 was the more sophisticated bar pickup with its notched blade and additional white binding. Christian played at least two ES150s and three ES250s, all of which had subtle differences. He also played, albeit less frequently, a Vega Electrolux (introduced in 1936), an Epiphone Electar (produced between 1935-1939) and early National and Harmony electrics (c. 1935-1939).

Because Christian was so closely associated with the Gibson ES150, literally dozens of would-be imitators went out and purchased the same model. By the late 30s, Gibson's first production line electric could be found in bands as diverse as the Bob Wills Texas Playboys, the King Cole Trio, Slim (Gaillard) and Slam (Stewart) and the Andy Kirk Orchestra.

5. Aaron T-Bone Walker

Charlie Christian's counterpart in blues, rhythm and blues, and the various offshoots of so-called 'race' music, was Aaron T-Bone Walker (1910-1975), a virtual contemporary and close friend of Christian's, who was also seduced by the sound and liberating potential of the electric guitar.

The music of T-Bone Walker (on Bleu 512)

T-Bone began playing the electric guitar in 1935, probably a Rickenbacker Vibrola model. He later recalled, 'It was kind of hard getting used to, because it had an echo sound. I would hit a string and hear the note behind me.' Like his friend, Walker soon obtained an early Gibson electric, a beautiful Sunburst ES250, which he kept until the late 1940s, when he exchanged it for an ES5, a guitar which marked a major move forward with its three pickups and modern cutaway shape.

Originally from Dallas, Texas, Walker learnt the basics of blues guitar playing from Blind Lemon Jefferson. Walker befriended Jefferson, to the extent that he helped him to collect tips and guided him around the streets of Dallas.

After experimenting with a variety of early electric guitars (c. 1935-1936), Walker played the fledgling instrument well enough to obtain a place in a number of Texas Swing bands, including the Lawson Brooks Band, a unit in which Charlie Christian was also to play at a later date. It was not until 1939, after T-Bone Walker had moved to Los Angeles and joined Les Hite's Cotton Club Band, that he recorded the classic *T-Bone Blues*.

The success of this first single enabled him to leave Hite's band in 1941, and go out on the road under his own name. By 1942, he was recording for Capitol and touring the length and breadth of the country. Unlike Charlie Christian, whose recording career was tragically limited by his early death, T-Bone continued recording until his debilitating stroke in 1974. Perhaps his greatest legacy, and best known work, was the tune *They Call it Stormy Monday*, first recorded in 1946, for the Black and White label and since covered by artists as diverse as Etta James, Eva Cassidy and Chris Farlow.

Besides his obvious skills as a guitarist, Walker was also a gifted singer and, perhaps more importantly, a great showman. His entertaining stage shows included tap dancing, doing the splits, playing the guitar behind his back and between his legs. Many of these antics were copied by Guitar Slim in the 1950s, and later by Chuck Berry and Jimi Hendrix among others. It might even be argued that the way in which Walker incorporated showmanship with performance, to heighten intensity and audience excitement, paved the way for the so-called 'guitar heroes', who emerged during the late 60s and are still a feature of some present-day rock bands. Strictly speaking, neither Charlie Christian nor T-Bone Walker were the first to record with the electric guitar. Their combined efforts, however, provided a focus which became the catalyst for the instrument's wider acceptance.

6. The Furtherance of the Electric Guitar

Other players who contributed to the furtherance of the electric guitar in an important, albeit less spectacular way, included George Barnes (1921-1977) who claimed to have played an electric guitar made by his brother in 1931.

George Barnes on the cover of BMG, January 1956

We do know that George Barnes purchased one of the first National/Dobro short scale solid-bodied electrics (c.1933), and was certainly among the first to play an electric guitar regularly on the radio. Later guitar celebrities such as Chet Atkins, Merle Travis, Roy Lanham and Herb Ellis cite Barnes's electric playing as an important early influence.

Eddie Durham (1906-1987) recorded the electric guitar in 1938, with the Kansas City Five. It was Durham who introduced Christian to the possibilities of the instrument when he passed through Oklahoma in 1937 and as such, played a significant role in the latter's transition from acoustic to electric guitar. In an interview with Frederic V. Grunfeld (1969), Durham recalled, 'He had big eyes to sound like a saxophone and I showed him how, by using downstrokes, he could get a sharper tone.'

Floyd Smith (1917-1982) was also an early advocate of the electric guitar, and was featured prominently with both electric Spanish and electric lap steel instruments during his stint with the Andy Kirk Band. His recording of *Floyd's Guitar Blues,* made in 1939, appears to have been very influential, despite the fact that it utilized the lap steel. Later versions of the same tune, however, were recorded on a regular six string electric guitar.

Although all these players furthered the popularity of the electric guitar through their inspired playing, it should be remembered that there were literally dozens of others who, due to various circumstances, were not as well known. It could be argued that these less famous participants were perhaps equally important in winning an audience for the electric guitar.

With the instrument still in its infancy during the years when Charlie Christian and T-Bone Walker made their impact, it was indeed the widespread acceptance and adoption of the electric guitar by a host of players now long-forgotten which eventually dispelled its former reputation as a musical novelty.

PART III: THE JAZZ AGE

7. Les Paul

During the 1940s and 50s the electric guitar underwent a tremendous surge in popularity. Recordings by Les Paul *(Lover)*, Arthur Smith *(Guitar Boogie)* and Johnny Smith *(Moonlight in Vermont)* firmly established the instrument's sound in popular culture, elevating it from the dark dissonance of bebop jazz to the more consonant textures of a rapidly developing style called western swing. While these genres in particular produced a number of excellent and influential guitar players, the pioneering work of Les Paul was musically more accessible, the results of which were far-reaching in their consequences.

Les Paul on the cover of BMG, July 1946

Les Paul (b. 1915) began playing the guitar in 1927. His initial interest lay in country music, but on hearing Eddie Lang and later Django Reinhardt, he set about developing a single-string technique which was not dissimilar in sound and style to the playing of his friend, and erstwhile rival, George Barnes. Like Barnes, Paul was also an early experimenter with the electric

23

guitar, fashioning a number of intriguing devices from home-made crystal sets. In fact his compulsive tinkering, and fascination with electronics, eventually led to a number of important breakthroughs in both multi-track recording and electric guitar technology.

The Les Paul Trio, (formed in 1937) made their first recordings in 1939. Following stints in New York and Chicago, the Trio moved to California where they worked and recorded with artists such as Bing Crosby, Helen Forrest and the Andrews Sisters. While in California, Paul converted his garage into a recording studio. By 1947, he had produced the multi-track recording of *Lover*, released by Capitol records a year later. The enormous success of *Lover* marked the beginning of a long and successful career in popular music. More importantly, it also launched the generic guitar sound which was to form the backbone of popular music for the next three decades. Les Paul's inimitable guitar playing was highly melodic, mischievous and virtuosic. Yet, like Paul himself, the music was never aloof or unapproachable.

He began his career when the electric guitar was in its infancy, playing acoustic Gibsons but soon changed to electric Epiphones. Throughout the 1940s most of his recordings were made on an early electric Epiphone archtop, which underwent more and more radical modifications with the passing years.

> I took that guitar and mounted pickups where I wanted to mount them and do what I wanted to do...The whole top was changed. It had a hole in the back of it and you could go in there and do whatever you wanted to do...I had soundposts in there; all kinds of things to make it sustain. I put plywood tops on it a half inch thick - no F holes; I tried all kinds of things.[1]

---

1.   Paul, L., 'Players In Their Own Words,' Fisch, J.,/Fred, L. B., *Epiphone: The House of Stathopoulo*, Amsco, 1996, p. 205.

Around 1940 Les Paul owned at least three Epiphone Zephyrs, all of which were subjected to various degrees of surgery. His most interesting experiment, however, was the groundbreaking Log.

During the late 30s, Les Paul took a 14 x 4 piece of solid pine and attached it to the end of a guitar neck. He then fitted two pickups, a bridge and a tailpiece to this primitive guitar body, in an attempt to prove that the solid-bodied guitar had a purer tone and better sustain than the amplified archtops of the time. Between 1940 and 1941, Paul took his creation in turn to Epiphone, Vega and Gibson, to demonstrate the viability of the solid-body guitar, hoping that someone would offer to manufacture an instrument based upon the precepts of his design. However, this was not to be. Paul was ridiculed. Instead Gibson, for example, called him 'the man with the broomstick with pickups on it'.

After encountering much prejudice and resistance, Les Paul decided to give the Log a more conventional guitar-like appearance, by building it into the body of a regular Epiphone archtop. Les Paul had not, strictly speaking, invented the solid-bodied guitar. Small-bodied, short scale instruments had, as we have already seen, been around since the early 30s. He did, however, demonstrate how the solid-body principle could be effectively applied to a regular full-scale instrument.

More importantly, Paul's early attempts to produce a full-size, solid-bodied instrument inadvertently resulted in one of the earliest known examples of a semi-acoustic guitar. While this was never his express intention, by adding clip-on acoustic sides to the Log, Les Paul had unwittingly provided the embryonic prototype from which instruments such as the Gibson ES335 were to evolve later. Ironically, Gibson did not produce their first solid-bodied electric guitar until 1952: the Gibson *Les Paul*! Their first semi-acoustic guitar - the ES335 - did not appear until 1958!

8. Fender and the Solid-Bodied Electric Guitar

There is some dispute as to who actually conceived and designed the first full-scale, solid-bodied electric guitar. In essence all post -1930s solids evolved from George Beauchamp's Rickenbackers. Establishing the precise date and the designer of the first solid-bodied version of a 'conventional' six string guitar is, however, more problematic. O. W. Appleton designed and built his 'APP' solid-body in 1941, which roughly corresponds with Les Paul's experiments with the 'Log'.

By the late 40s, two more names had entered the arena: Paul Bigsby and Leo Fender. The popular Country and Western guitarist, Merle Travis (1917-83), designed an early solid-body guitar, the specifications for which included a single cutaway and single-sided machine heads, features which later became synonymous with the design of Fender guitars. Merle asked his friend, Paul Bigsby, to build a guitar based upon his futuristic design, which he subsequently played on many gigs. Travis later claimed that Leo Fender had borrowed the Bigsby/Travis guitar for a week, during which time he built a similar instrument. In truth we will never know for certain who was the real pioneer, but Fender's instruments proved the most successful and his name will always be the one most closely associated with the birth of the solid-body guitar.

Leo Fender started out in the musical instrument business in 1945, with friend and co-designer Doc Kauffman. At first, their company, K and F, built lap steels and amplifiers. When K and F folded in 1946, Leo set up alone, working for the first time, under the auspicious 'Fender' name.

Leo Fender went on to market successfully the solid-body electric guitar, firstly with the single pickup Esquire and twin pickup Broadcaster, and later with the ever popular three-pickup Stratocaster. The Broadcaster underwent a temporary name change when it became the No-caster, before acquiring its now famous 'Telecaster' moniker.

The more radical and futuristically shaped Stratocaster, did not appear until the spring of 1954. Both models have since become icons - the very personification of the electric guitar. The popularity of these instruments has been so great that they have remained in continuous production ever since their inception, seducing each new generation of players with their curvaceous bodies and tonal versatility.

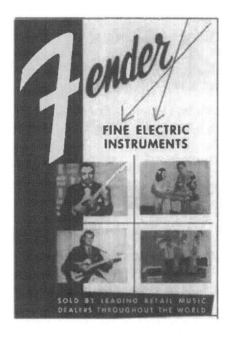

The Fender Catalog of 1955

Early Fender players, and endorsees include Jimmy Bryant, Bill Carson, Arthur Smith, Alvino Rey and Buddy Merrill (who was featured weekly on the Lawrence Welk TV show playing early Fender solid-body guitars).

Originally, Fender guitars were the most popular among Country players, especially those with strong jazz leanings such as Jimmy Bryant, whose 1955 recording *Two Guitars Country Style* (with steel guitarist Speedy West), helped to put the Fender Telecaster on the map.

Jimmy Bryant and Speedy West (with Johnny Dennis)
at the KXLA (California) Broadcasting Studios (BMG, June, 1955)

In the same period, guitarists such as Jimmy Wyble and Eldon Shamblin played boppish leads and jazz chords on their Stratocasters, with Bob Wills and the Texas Playboys, while Thumbs Carlile played jazzy fills behind the popular country singer, Roger Miller.

For the most part, jazz guitarists continued to play Gibson or Epiphone full-bodied electrics. A substantial number of jazz players also continued to use traditional archtop acoustics from the same makers, as well as those produced by master luthiers such as John D'Angelico (1905-1964) and Elmer Stromberg (1895-1955).

9. Pickups and Archtops

Since the early 1940s, various companies had manufactured attachable 'after-market' pickups. These included the short-lived Rickenbacker S-59 (introduced in 1941), which clipped to the table and ribs of the guitar, via an adjustable screw and thread system, similar to those used for violin chin rests, and the DeArmond FCH-Guitar Mike (introduced in 1942) which clamped to the strings behind the bridge, and was held rigid by a long metal rod. The popular DeArmond pickup underwent several basic transformations, but continued to retain its original clamping system, which meant it could be used without any modification to the guitar.

Many guitarists who required both an electric and acoustic instrument chose the acoustic archtop, with the detachable DeArmond option. Among the jazz players who did so were Johnny Smith (D'Angelico), John Pisano (D'Angelico), Irving Ashby (Stromberg), Billy Bauer (D'Angelico), Django Reinhardt (Maccaferri with Stima pickup), Arv Garrison (Gibson L5) and Bill DeArango (Gibson Super 400).

Other important jazz guitarists preferred to play proprietary brand electric archtops, from such companies as Gibson (Tal Farlow, Jimmy Raney, Barney Kessel), Epiphone (Chuck Wayne, Al Caiola, Billy Bean) and Gretsch (Sal Salvador, Mary Osborne, Bill Jennings).

10. A Significant Solo Voice

During the decade between 1946 and 1956, the electric guitar became well established as a significant solo voice in modern jazz. Motivated largely by Charlie Christian's horn-like improvisations, and Oscar Moore's lush chords, an entire generation of jazz guitarists consolidated and furthered the endeavors of their predecessors. The most successful of these obtained work with prominent,well-respected leaders, and in so doing gained valuable exposure.

Oscar Moore's Correspondence Course in guitar playing

Between 1946 and 1952, for example, Chuck Wayne (1923-1997) was with pianist George Shearing, playing his guitar in the low, or middle register, of tightly arranged close-harmony chords. The resulting timbre, known as the 'Shearing sound', was very popular and therefore widely imitated.

During these years, there were literally hundreds of fine jazz guitarists in the USA and a growing number overseas. Many remained unknown outside their home towns and others, such as Ronnie Singer (Chicago), Bill Dillard (Los Angeles), Pete Chilvers and Dave Goldberg (England) were known and appreciated by other musicians but failed to reach a wider audience.

Around the same time, Jimmy Raney (1927-1995) demonstrated how well the electric guitar also blended with the tenor saxophone, while playing with the popular Stan Getz Quintet. Recordings by these groups were hugely influential, creating models for others to copy.

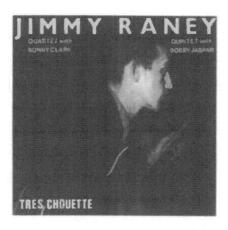

Jimmy Raney (on Vogue VG651)

Few jazz guitarists, however, have been as influential as Tal Farlow (1921-1998) whose iconoclastic recordings, with the Red Norvo Trio, lifted the instrument onto a higher plateau both technically and harmonically. Farlow had a precociously facile technique, and an adventurous harmonic sense to match. His virtuosic lines mirrored the innovative saxophone improvisations of Charlie Parker, while his chording was as complex and futuristic as any modern pianist of the day.

31

Tal Farlow provided a vital link, in the development of jazz guitar improvisation, bridging the gap between Charlie Christian and those who were to follow, such as Wes Montgomery and Joe Pass.

Tal Farlow's Promotional Postcard

Other major jazz players of the period who helped to win a wider audience for the electric guitar included Barney Kessel (b. 1923), who was the first to record jazz guitar with the skeletal support of bass and drums, and Johnny Smith, whose 1952 recording of *Moonlight in Vermont* (with saxophonist Stan Getz) proved to be a huge success.

Johnny Smith featured on the Guild Brochure, 1953-1955

The electric guitar had made unprecedented progress, during the decade between 1946 and 1956, primarily as a result of a handful of gifted jazz players coupled with the technological advances made by innovators such as Les Paul and Leo Fender. This progress was, however, tiny by comparison with the momentous changes which lay ahead.

PART IV: ROCK'N'ROLL

11. Bill Haley and Rock'n'Roll

In 1951, Bill Haley (1925-1981) recorded *Rocket 88*, an early, albeit rudimentary, rock'n'roll tune. If this event passed with little ceremony, Haley's 1954 recording of *Rock Around the Clock*, heralded the birth of rock'n'roll, a musical genre in which the guitar was soon to become an indispensable sound, prop, fashion statement and design icon.

Bill Haley featured in The History of Rock

With the advent of rock'n'roll, the acoustic steel-string guitar had turned into something of a dinosaur, used primarily by singer/songwriters such as Woody Guthrie and Ramblin' Jack Elliott, exponents of, and specialists in Bluegrass, Country Blues, and other North American ethnic musics (Doc Watson, Lester Flatt, Brownie McGhee, Big Bill Broonzy et al.). In popular

34

music the role of the acoustic guitar mirrored that previously occupied by its electric counterpart in that it was called upon solely for specific tonal colors and rhythmic effects.

Prompted, in part, by the specter of rock'n'roll, and further encouraged by the unexpected success of the Fender Telecaster, Gibson approached Les Paul to design a signature model solid-body guitar. By the early 50s, Paul was riding the crest of commercial prosperity, following the popular appeal of instrumentals such as *Lover, Caravan* and *Nola*, as well as the chart-topping achievement of *How High The Moon* with his wife, the vocalist Mary Ford.

Les Paul and Mary Ford (BMG, April 1956)

Having the weight of a well-known guitar player behind their initial foray into an uncharted area, gave Gibson's Managing Directors the confidence they had lacked when previously approached by the 'broomstick man'. Even so, the Les Paul guitar was carefully designed to look like a smaller version of their archtops, right down to the curvature of the arched maple top and traditional-style, raised pickguard.

Les Paul Flametop (c.1958)

Gibson's first solid-body was launched in 1952, at the height of Les Paul's recording career. It sold extremely well at first, but by 1960 sales had fallen to such a degree that the Les Paul design was phased out - eventually to be re-introduced by popular demand, in 1968. Despite their earliest associations with 'mainstream' country (Fender), and jazz (Gibson), solid-body electric guitars had by the late 50s, become synonymous with high-volume, high-energy rock music; an association which has continued to this day.

12. A Multiplicity of Styles

By the 1950s the electric guitar had been absorbed into most styles of popular music. In each case the lineage could be traced back through an increasing number of players to a handful of early pioneers. In modern jazz, for instance, the electric guitar had travelled from the raw energy of Charlie Christian to the harmonic sophistication of Tal Farlow and Barney Kessel.

Playing styles appear to have subdivided into country music, producing fingerpickers (Merle Travis and Chet Atkins), and flatpickers (Jimmy Bryant, Hank Garland and Joe Maphis). Blues music grew increasingly urbane, typified by the electric guitar-based music emanating from black ghettos on the south side of Chicago. The electric guitar was also well represented in commercial popular music by Les Paul, Al Caiola, Tony Mottola (a regular performer on the Perry Como Show) and George Barnes.

Each style produced its figureheads. Such players were usually able to synthesize elements of previous stylists, and in doing so, add something of their own which held wide appeal. Rock'n'roll was perhaps the best example of this 'melting pot' drawing from a rich but complex matrix of country, blues and jazz. The early examples were little more than pastiche, born from the cross-fertilization of North American guitar-based cultures and Afro-American traditions. Such eclecticism was effectively described by Elvis Presley's guitarist, Scotty Moore, when listing his early influences in a *Guitar Player* interview (August, 1974):

> I was listening to Atkins, Travis, Barney Kessel, Tal Farlow, B. B. King. I was just into everybody. As long as he played guitar he was fine with me.

The 1950s witnessed a rapid growth of youth culture. Teenagers found a new sense of identity, which was frequently based upon the idealized roles of film stars like Marlon Brando (*The Wild One*) and James Dean (*Rebel Without a Cause*). The music of Bill Haley, Elvis Presley, Jerry Lee Lewis and Gene Vincent, further alienated parents, and thus gained popularity among teenagers virtually overnight. Electric guitars formed the backbone of this 'new' music and were unjustifiably considered to be 'instruments of the Devil' by many worried parents.

Rock Around the Clock, recorded in 1954 by Bill Haley and the Comets, may not have been the first, but it was certainly the most successful rock'n'roll record of its day. It gained wide exposure when MGM featured the tune both on the soundtrack of the movie *The Blackboard Jungle*, and, a year later, in the film *Rock Around the Clock*.

37

Haley's popularity helped to establish the 12-bar blues progression, with obligatory guitar solo, as the principal rock'n'roll vehicle, creating a model which virtually defined the genre. His regular guitarist, Frannie Beecher (b.1922) was a fine jazz player, who had previously worked with clarinetist Benny Goodman. It was Danny Cedrone, however, and not Beecher who played the intricate jazzy solo on *Rock Around the Clock*.

13. The Influence of Elvis Presley

If Haley's music became a catalyst in the search for youth identity, his personal image was rather staid; a little too sober to become a pervasive role model for teenagers. That privilege fell to Elvis Presley, whose 1956 recording of *Heartbreak Hotel* sold over a million copies in its first week.

Presley's moody vocals, and guitarist Scotty Moore's earthy solos, owed more to the blues musicians of Memphis, Texas and Chicago than to the relatively tame, rock'n' roll posturing of Bill Haley. Haley's guitarist played his black Gibson Les Paul Custom with sophistication and taste. By contrast, Moore's style had a rawness which captured the primal essence and latent energy of the new music. He had ingeniously borrowed the call and response (voice and guitar) approach of B. B. King and T-Bone Walker, married this with Merle Travis's fingerpicking style and doused the results with liberal helpings of echo, resulting in an 'electric' tone previously associated with Les Paul. This style, which became known as rockabilly, inspired and encouraged literally thousands of young hopefuls to take up the guitar.

Rock'n'roll was destined to become a multi-billion dollar industry, and the electric guitar an integral part of it. Slowly but surely, the idea of a group, whose line-up included drums, bass, lead and rhythm guitar, took shape. Several popular groups also included pianists or saxophonists, but the general trend was towards guitar dominated units like Gene Vincent and the Blue Caps, and Buddy Holly and the Crickets.

This format was widely copied, not only in the USA, but elsewhere, especially England where rock'n'roll quickly took hold. Early British imitations included Tommy Steele and the Steelemen, Joe Brown and his Bruvvers, Marty Wilde and the Wild Cats, Johnny Kidd and the Pirates and the most influential of all early British rock groups, Cliff Richard and the Shadows.

Following in the wake of Scotty Moore's inspirational playing with Elvis Presley, Cliff Richard's several other 'backing' guitarists proved influential in furthering the popularity of the electric guitar. Most notable figures were James Burton (b.1939), (his winning Fender Telecaster adorned recordings by Dale Hawkins and Ricky Nelson), and Cliff Gallop (1935-1988), whose recordings with Gene Vincent made a lasting impression upon Jeff Beck, Albert Lee and Richie Blackmoore.

A little more obscure, but no less influential was Paul Burlison (b.1929), whose raucous, distorted Fender Esquire almost qualified Johnny Burnette's epochal Rock'n'Roll Trio as the first heavy metal group!

14. Chuck Berry

Besides these early, but notable, band members were several singer-guitarists, whose more overt exploitation of the electric guitar won over new audiences. Eddie Cochran (1938-1960), Buddy Holly (1936-1959) and Chuck Berry (b.1926) must, by any criterion, be viewed as important electric guitar players.

From the memorable opening guitar licks of *Maybellene* in 1955 to the guitar solos in *Roll Over Beethoven*, *Johnny B. Goode* and *Carol*, Chuck Berry's guitar style has been copied by thousands. During the early 60s, it was mandatory for every self-respecting rock guitarist to emulate his solos note for note. When rock'n'roll eventually subsided into the so-called 'Beat Boom', Chuck Berry's records provided would-be electric guitarists with some of their most important lessons:

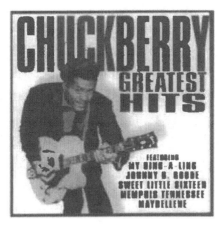

A reissue of Chuck Berry favorites on PLATCD 235

CHUCK BERRY'S INFLUENTIAL 1950s RECORDINGS

1955	*MAYBELLENE/Wee Wee Hours*	Chess 1604
	Thirty Days/Together	Chess 1610
1956	*No Money Down/Down Bound Train*	Chess 1615
	ROLL OVER BEETHOVEN/Drifting Heart	Chess 1626
	Brown Eyed Handsome Man/TOO MUCH	
	MONKEY BUSINESS	Chess 1635
	You Can't Catch Me/Havana Moon	Chess 1645
1957	*School Day/Deep Feeling*	Chess 1653
	Oh Baby Doll/La Juanda	Chess 1664
	ROCK'N'ROLL MUSIC/Blue Feeling	Chess 1671
	JOHNNY B. GOODE/AROUND + AROUND	Chess 1691
	BEAUTIFUL DELILAH/Vacation Time	Chess 1697
	CAROL/Hey Pedro	Chess 1700
	Sweet Little Rock'n'Roller/Jo Jo Gunne	Chess 1709
	Run Rudolph Run/Merry Christmas Baby	Chess 1714
1959	*Anthony Boy/That's My Desire*	Chess 1716
	Almost Grown/LITTLE QUEENIE	Chess 1722
	BACK IN THE USA/MEMPHIS TENNESSEE	Chess 1729
	Childhood Sweetheart/Broken Arrow	Chess 1737

[Upper case titles are those which proved the most influential.]

Berry's style owed much to blues guitarists, especially Guitar Slim and T-Bone Walker. Walker, Slim and George Barnes (a session player on many blues recordings, who advocated the use of a plain 3rd (G) string in his *Modern Guitar Method* of 1943), had all discovered that by discarding the 6th string (E), and moving the remaining strings down one, and then substituting a thinner banjo string for the top E, the resulting lighter gauge (with three unwound strings) enabled them to bend strings.

A "bend" is executed by fingering a fret below the note to be played; then pushing the string across the neck, tightening it until the intended note sounds.

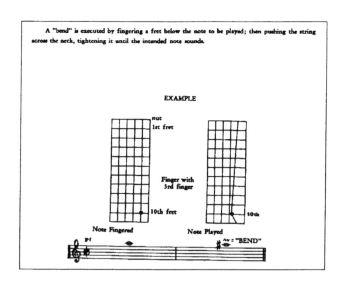

EXAMPLE

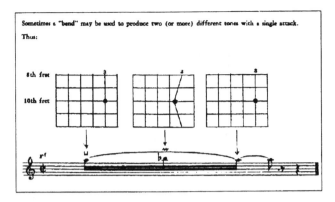

George Barnes in his Guitar Method of 1943 explaining the technique of the Bend.

Blues guitarists had been doing this for years, but it was the early rock'n'roll players like Chuck Berry and James Burton who popularized the wider use of this practice. Light gauge strings, with unwound thirds, however, were not commercially available until the introduction of Fender's Rock'n'Roll set (Number 150) in the early 60s.

15. New Guitars and Amplifiers

As the popularity of rock'n'roll grew into a youth obsession, manufacturers of electric guitars and amplifiers began to enjoy a corresponding boom in sales. New models were introduced with increased regularity and factory floors were extended in an attempt to meet the additional demand for instruments.

Whereas Gibson and Fender had previously been the major source for electric guitars, other more traditional marques like Epiphone, Gretsch, Rickenbacker, Harmony and Kay now began to produce instruments they felt would appeal to the burgeoning rock'n'roll market. In order to remain competitive, companies began to introduce new updated models such as Fender's 1958 Jazzmaster and Gibson's so-called 'modernistic' series which included the Flying V and Explorer (both 1958).

43

Budget models were also introduced, aimed expressly at younger players. These guitars had ¾ size bodies and short scale fingerboards to accommodate smaller hands. (Fender's ¾ size Duo-Sonic and Musicmaster (1956), Gibson's Les Paul Junior ¾ (1956), ES140 ¾ (1957), Melody Maker (1959) and Rickenbacker's thinline hollowbody 310-325 series (1958) were among this proliferation of diminutive guitars for diminutive players.)

Most manufacturers also followed Fender's and Gibson's example and were, by the mid 50s, producing solid-body guitars. Gretsch, like Gibson, a company previously associated with fine quality acoustic archtops, were among the first, with their Les Paul look-alikes the 'Duo Jet' (1953), 'Round-Up' (1954), 'Chet Atkins Solid-Body' (1955) and luxurious top of the range 'White Penguin' (1955). Notable advocates of these guitars included Cliff Gallop, Bo Diddley, Chet Atkins, Chuck Berry (before he switched to Gibson), and a little later, George Harrison. Gretsch's electric archtops, especially the bright orange or red 6120 models, were used to great effect by Eddie Cochran, Duane Eddy and Sid Manker, the guitarist featured on Bill Justis's 1957 hit *Raunchy*.

Other brands of electric guitars popular among rock'n'roll players included Guild (Charlie Gracie, Duane Eddy, Jorgen Ingmann), Epiphone (Hank Garland, Billy Butler) and a variety of cheaper 'entry level' instruments by Kay, Harmony, National, Danelectro and Premier.

16. The Guitar in Europe

For logistical reasons, the European scenario was somewhat different. Until 1960 there had been a post-war trade embargo on USA imports, which made it virtually impossible to buy American-made electric guitars in Europe. Yet, as a result of the rock'n'roll revolution, electric guitars were in great demand in Europe which naturally led to a plethora of domestically manufactured instruments, predominantly of Eastern European origin.

The most popular of these were undoubtedly those manufactured by Hofner, which were imported into England during the late 50s and early 60s. Virtually all of England's early rock stars such as Tommy Steele, Marty Wilde and Billy Fury, played Hofner guitars, as did Bert Weedon, whose 1959 record *Guitar Boogie Shuffle* was the first guitar-centered instrumental to enter the British charts.

Bert Weedon featured in BMG, October 1960

Hank Marvin, Albert Lee, Richie Blackmore, Phil Manzanera, Bernie Marsden, Tom McGuinness and Steve Winwood were among the thousands of British youngsters for whom a Hofner became a stepping-stone to greater things. Other electric guitar makes popular with early British rock'n'roll players, included Futurama (Czechoslovakia), Guyatone (Japan), Rosetti (Holland), Watkins, Vox and Burns (England).

17. Duane Eddy and the Twang

In less than a decade, rock'n'roll had earned the electric guitar a universal appeal, its popularity had spread to virtually every corner of the globe. Yet, while guitar groups from such unlikely places as Sweden (the Sputniks) achieved notoriety, North America remained the focal point in the electric guitar's development. Paradoxically, at the very time when the format of singer with backing instruments had become firmly established, a new breed of guitar soloist appeared. These guitarists used their instrument to play complete melodies, rather than short breaks, a role previously reserved for the singer.

Further exploiting the electric guitar's strident sound, individuals like Duane Eddy, Chet Atkins, Link Wray and Dick Dale, together with instrumental groups the Ventures, Surfaris and Shadows, collectively ensured that the electric guitar was *the* predominant sound in popular music.

Duane Eddy (b.1938), the first commercially packaged guitar instrumentalist, was nurtured and marketed by Lee Hazlewood who co-wrote, arranged and produced Eddy's early hits. Hazlewood was also responsible for developing Eddy's signature 'twangy' sound, which relied upon a combination of bass strings and echo, together with ambient handclaps and background yells.

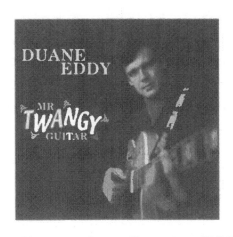

Duane Eddy - a compilation of his music on PLS CD 309

Although Eddy's recordings were extremely simplistic and well within the reach of any guitar-playing novice, he had, in fact, studied with Jimmy Wyble and Al Casey. It was whilst recording with Casey, in Phoenix, that the basis of his twangy sound was discovered. Hazlewood was producing the session, and on hearing some of Eddy's low register backing figures decided to re-record the tune bringing out these low register figures. The resulting *Moovin'N'Groovin'* was a minor hit. The twang laden *Rebel Rouser*, released a short time later, sold over a million copies.

Like Eddie Cochran and Chet Atkins, Duane Eddy used a big-bodied Gretsch 6120, an instrument which he played until 1962, when Guild manufactured their Duane Eddy signature model.

18. Chet Atkins and Gretsch Guitars

The artist most associated with Gretsch guitars, during the 50s, was the multi-talented Chet Atkins (b.1924). Both in his appearance and mannerisms, Atkins stood a world apart from rock'n'roll culture. A staid, quiet personality, with almost aristocratic bearing, Chet Atkins became known as the 'Country Gentleman', an honorary title that Gretsch, appropriately, also used for the 17" signature guitar launched in 1957.

Chet Atkins (BMG, September 1963)

Atkins worked closely with Gretsch, and played a major part in popularizing their electric guitars. Unusually, however, he was responsible for a Chet Atkins series of instruments rather than any one specific model. These included the 1955 Chet Atkins solid-body, the popular 6120, followed by the Chet Atkins Country Gentleman (1957) and Tennessean (1959).

These guitars marked a significant upturn in the fortunes of the Gretsch company, whose early electrics had been unable to compete with Fender and Gibson. With the appearance of the Atkins series, Gretsch guitars began to play a major part in the development of rock'n'roll, as evidenced by the playing of Cochran, Gallop, Eddy and later, a young George Harrison!

If not a role model for the rebellious youth of the late 50s, Atkins was nevertheless enigmatic. His playing had evolved from the alternating bass, with melody on top, Travis picking. Unlike Merle Travis, however, whose music was steeped in the tradition of Country, Bluegrass and Western Swing, Atkins diluted the more overt stylistic aspects. By reducing Travis's blistering, bluegrass style workouts to a simple bass line with a melody on top, Chet Atkins developed an approach which was altogether more direct. Because the resulting effect sounded uncannily like two people playing together, Atkins became an early guitar hero with a massive influence on the younger generation.

Chet Atkins in the Gretsch Catalog, 1955

Like the majority of jazz and classical musicians, he achieved popularity through LP recordings rather than huge selling hit singles. Tunes like *Trambone, Windy and Warm* and the teasingly deceptive *Yankee Doodle Plays a Fugue* became standard tests of accomplishment for fledgling guitarists. If Scotty Moore, Cliff Gallop and James Burton were at the forefront of the 'first wave' of influential rock'n'roll guitarists, Chet Atkins and Chuck Berry spearheaded the second.

19. The Golden Age of Electric Guitar Design

It was predominantly as a result of these players that the electric guitar entered the 1960s with newfound popularity. Both the Shadows and the Ventures were riding high in the pop charts with guitar instrumentals; Duane Eddy, Jorgen Ingmann, Bert Weedon, Dick Dale et al., were also putting the guitar further out front with their successful, albeit diverse, instrumental recordings.

Guitar sales too were up on previous years. Many players and collectors now consider the late 50s, and early 60s, to be the 'golden age' of electric guitar design and manufacture. Indeed, Gibson's semi-acoustic, thinline ES335 range, launched in the spring of 1958, was certainly one of their crowning achievements. So too was the 1958-1960 variant of the Les Paul Standard, with its gorgeous flame maple top and cherry Sunburst finish.

These were also prime years for Fender, with the introduction of the top-of-the-line 'Jazzmaster' (1958) and standardization of custom color finishes (1958-1965). Epiphone, a company which had been bought out by Gibson in 1957, launched a series of popular thinlines which closely resembled the ES335 range, while Gretsch expanded their Chet Atkins range along with several new models not carrying the 'signature' endorsement. Electric guitars, by all of these companies, plus many more, were finding their way into households all over the world, soon to become an integral part of the 'Swingin' 60s'.

Gibson Catalog (early 1960s) showing Electric Spanish Guitars (Thin Models)

PART V: THE SWINGIN' 60s

20. The Early 60s

Like any popular fad, rock'n'roll was to prove short-lived. The music evolved in a number of directions but generally gravitated away from the 'three chord trick' (I-IV-V) towards a more melodic and harmonically varied style. By 1962, many of the major rock'n'roll figures had either tragically died (Buddy Holly and Eddie Cochran) or been restrained, the best examples being the drafting of Elvis Presley into the US army (1958-1960) and the incarceration of Chuck Berry (1962-1964).

Duane Eddy's late 50s and early 60s guitar instrumentals, *Rebel Rouser* (1958), *Because They're Young* and *Peter Gunn* (1960) fuelled a trend, and there was a plethora of best selling singles released between 1958 and 1964. Characterized by their surprising variety, these instrumentals encompassed a number of disparate approaches - from clean, melodic, soft-rock tunes by the Shadows (*Apache, F.B.I., Man of Mystery,* etc.) and the Ventures (*Walk Don't Run, Perfidia, Ram-Bunk-Shush,* etc.) to the earthy, more raucous, sounds of Link Wray (*The Rumble*) and the Surfaris (*Wipe Out*).

There was humor too, as evidenced by such frivolities as *Nut Rocker* (B. Bumble and the Stingers), *Rocking Goose* and *Reveille Rock* (Johnny and the Hurricanes) and in England, *Hoots Mon* by Lord Rockingham's XI.

Despite such diversity, or maybe even as a result of it, the recordings by guitar-based groups were the most formulaic, principal models being the Ventures in the USA, and the Shadows in England. Both groups produced a clean, refined sound, heightened by judicious use of echo.

Their considered presentation of a catchy melody was virtually an updated variation of Les Paul's 1940s and early 50s recordings, but whereas Paul had used novel multitrack techniques, to create the illusion of speed and ensemble, both the Ventures and the Shadows relied upon simple monothematic melodies with a rhythmic backdrop. Extensive use of the tremolo arm (or 'whammy bar' as it later became known) gave these melodies the necessary contemporary flavor.

Hank Marvin of the Shadows featured on the back cover of Beat, July 1963

This ubiquitous formula established the classic line-up of four players, each with a specific role: an electric bassist, drummer and two guitars. The guitars were further sub-divided into lead and rhythm, literal designations which were seldom to be crossed.

Both groups played Fenders, providing hitherto unprecedented publicity for their electric guitars, not only through their concerts and TV broadcasts, but also LP sleeves, magazine articles and promotional material. Suddenly, the Fender Stratocaster was at the top of every young boy's 'wants' list, the stuff of which dreams are, and indeed were, made!

Bob Bogle and Hank Marvin popularized the electric guitar to a degree unimaginable in the 1950s, building on the earlier groundwork of Gallop, Moore, Atkins and Eddy. The rather less genteel influence of Chuck Berry and Chicago blues, however, did not show up until a little later, when bands like the Rolling Stones and the Yardbirds spearheaded a new, albeit guitar-based movement.

By 1962, the electric guitar had become the face of popular music. Besides its substantial role in the charts, it was also prominent in TV programmes like *Bonanza* as well as in blockbuster films such as *Doctor No*, the first in a succession of James Bond movies which made extensive use of the electric guitar.

21. Guitar Methods

There was, of course, a corresponding increase in sales of didactic material, with a number of new publications directed at the thousands of would-be pop stars. Despite the appearance of books aimed specifically at the youth market (such as Roger Filiberto's *Teenage Guitar)*, Ronny Lee's *Rock'n'Roll Guitar Book*, and Dick Sadleir's *Rhythm & Blues Guitar* and more traditional fare continued to prove the most popular and, it could be argued, most effective. Mel Bay's *Modern Guitar Method*, Mickey Baker's *Jazz and Hot Guitar Course*, Sal Salvador's *Single Line Studies* (USA), Bert Weedon's seminal *Play in a Day* and Ivor Mairants's *Daily Scales and Exercises* (both UK) were also widely used.

Bert Weedon's Guitar Guide to Modern Guitar Playing - Play in a Day

Sheet music and tutors by the Shadows and the Ventures, including the forward thinking series *Play Guitar with the Ventures* (recordings with supporting tutorial material), nurtured the latent talent and enthusiasm of countless future guitar players.

22. Instrumentals

It was soon blatantly obvious that the curious, young guitarophile would not be satisfied with merely copying Hank Marvin or Bob Bogle ad infinitum. Once the degree of proficiency necessary to do so had been obtained, other horizons opened up. Perhaps the biggest failing, or weakness, of instrumental recordings like *Apache* and *Walk Don't Run* was their rigidity, the lack of opportunity for real self-expression.

Consequently, many electric guitar enthusiasts started to dig a little deeper, discovering the improvisation-based instrumentals of Freddie King (*Hide Away*), Albert Collins (*Frosty*) and of course, the instrumental B sides from Chuck Berry's popular singles on the Chess label (*Roly-Poly*, *Berry Picking*, *Low Feeling*, etc.).

Ultimately, instrumentals were destined to become little more than a novelty, a brief diversion from the singer with backing group format. The ephemeral sound of electric guitars, per se, went on to become an integral part of film and TV soundtracks, but apart from later arbitrary hits like Fleetwood Mac's *Albatross*, guitar instrumentals featured primarily on B sides or albums. Instrumental groups did, however, serve to establish the two guitars with drums, and electric bass line-up. When groups like the Shadows and the Ventures began to lose favor, the designated roles of lead and rhythm guitarist grew somewhat anachronistic, especially when band members were increasingly required to share vocal duties.

23. The New Guitarists of the 60s

In the early 60s, when a member of a 'pop' group was available on practically every street, there were not one but two generations of young guitarists - those who had come up through rock'n'roll and were already playing the dance halls and youth clubs, and those aspiring players, who, having mastered the Shadows/Ventures repertoire, were often turning to rhythm and blues.

An entirely new breed of jazz guitarists also emerged during the early 60s, most noticeably Joe Pass, Grant Green, Wes Montgomery and Kenny Burrell. Most of these exceptional players had, in fact, been working for years in the comparative obscurity of the jazz circuit. International recognition came late with the release of important albums such as, *Grant's*

First Stand - Blue Note (Grant Green), *Catch Me* - Pacific Jazz 73 (Joe Pass), *The Incredible Jazz Guitar of Wes Montgomery* - Riverside 320 and *Midnight Blue* - Blue Note 4123 (Kenny Burrell).

Players who were well established during the 1950s, like Johnny Smith, Barney Kessel, Herb Ellis, Chuck Wayne and Jimmy Raney, were still active but had slipped into relative obscurity. In many cases their recordings had either been deleted from the catalogs, or were difficult to obtain due to poor distribution.

Nevertheless, Gibson felt that the time was ripe to introduce three signature model electric archtops: the Johnny Smith and Barney Kessel (1961) and the Tal Farlow (1962). None of these instruments featured any radical design innovations, although for a deep-bodied jazz guitar, the Barney Kessel was unusual, in that it utilized a double-cutaway shape more usually associated with the solid-bodied guitar.

24. Wes Montgomery

Of all the jazz guitarists to win critical acclaim during the 1960s, Wes Montgomery (1923-1968) made the greatest impact. Montgomery developed the unorthodox technique of striking the strings with the fleshy ball of his right hand thumb, rather than the more customary practice of using a flat-pick. The resulting velvet tone was further thickened by his penchant for doubling melodies and single-line improvisations with another note, an octave above or below.

The virtuosic level to which this technique was developed remains awesome to this day and Montgomery's influence has been far-reaching, not only among other jazz guitarists, but also on electric guitarists in general. Octave passages in the style of Wes Montgomery, have since found their way into countless pop tunes. By 1968, Montgomery had become the first jazz guitarist to be awarded two gold discs but, sadly, died in June of that year, before he could reap the full benefits of his success.

Wes Montgomery

Grant Green and Kenny Burrell, were never as commercially successful as Wes Montgomery, but nevertheless made their mark, particularly in bluesy recordings with Hammond organists, Jimmy Smith and Jack McDuff. Joe Pass, however, still plagued by his earlier problems with heroin addiction, had to wait until the mid 70s before his precocious talents were fully appreciated. Apart from the incongruous blending of ethnic Hungarian music with early 50s bebop (Gabor Szabo), jazz guitar changed little until the late 60s, and the appearance of fusionists Larry Coryell and John McLaughlin.

25. The Electric Guitar and Country Music

Building on the earlier jazz-tinged playing of Jimmy Bryant, the electric guitar was also making headway in country music. Two of the leading figures were Don Rich (1941-1974) and Roy Nichols. Rich played with singer Buck

Owens's backing group, the Buckaroos, and was featured prominently on the instrumental recording appropriately titled *Buckaroo*. Nichols was the guitarist with Merle Haggard's Strangers, during which time he developed an influential Fender Telecaster-based style called chicken-pickin'.

Collectively, their incisive trebly tone, both courtesy of Fender Telecasters, became know as the 'Bakersfield Sound', a term which separated their style from the more polished and comparatively staid music emanating from Nashville at the time. Both Rich and Nichols, made more use of string bending than their predecessors, producing a sound which mimicked the pedal-steel. Now a part of the genre, the 'signature' licks of both players have been widely copied, finding their way into the styles of later greats such as Albert Lee, Roy Buchanan, Danny Gatton and Jerry Donahue.

26. The Beatles

Popular music, during the 1960s, was characterized by two things 'Beatlemania' and the 'British Invasion', both inextricably related to the unprecedented popularity of the electric guitar. It was at the height of the rock'n'roll era, in 1957, that John Lennon invited fellow guitarist/singer, Paul McCartney, to join the Quarrymen. Initially playing covers of Chuck Berry, Little Richard and the Everly Brothers, the Quarrymen were just one of the many 'beat' groups formed as a direct result of the electric guitar's recently acquired rock'n'roll identity.

Debuting in 1961, and settling down to the world-famous line-up in 1962, the success of the Beatles was nothing short of phenomenal. This multi-talented, guitar-based quartet irrevocably changed the face of popular music, repercussions of which were felt on many levels.

In the beginning the Beatles communicated an amateur enthusiasm coupled with the raw energy of rock'n'roll. Despite this 'common touch', their collective creativity and inquisitiveness ultimately enabled them to free popular music from the confines of the three minute single. The epic expanses of 'concept' albums, like *Sgt. Pepper's Lonely Hearts Club Band* (1967), marked a new epoch in popular music, paving the way for even greater self-expression.

With its eclectic, and forward-looking mix of styles from psychedelia to 1930s kitsch, *Sgt. Pepper's Lonely Hearts Club Band* was a milestone recording which had a huge influence upon things to come. Indeed, everything the Beatles did had some influence on the future direction of pop music, from guitarist George Harrison's use of the sitar, in 1965, to spearheading the 'British Invasion' of the USA, which opened the floodgates for greater convergence of Anglo-American styles.

The Beatles - 'Sgt. Pepper's Lonely Hearts Club Band' Album of 1967

By 1963, the Beatles were the obvious successors to Cliff Richard and the Shadows, heirs to the British rock'n'roll throne. Their more vital delivery of American, rock-influenced music circumvented the polished, and arguably sterile, packaging which had entrapped the competition. It was inevitable, upon the release of *Love Me Do* (1962) and even more so with *Please, Please Me* (1963), that the instrumental music of the Ventures or Shadows, together with the singer and backing band, rock'n'roll format had become deeply anachronistic.

Ironically, despite their move away from purely instrumental music, the Beatles had a stronger influence upon the sales of electric guitars than anyone ever before or since. Prior to the Beatles's 1964 appearance on the Ed Sullivan Show, Gibson and Fender had held a virtual monopoly on high volume guitar sales (excepting the budget-line instruments by Harmony and Kay). George Harrison's choice of instrument, the Gretsch 'Country Gentleman', gave this New York company the best endorsement that they could wish for. Correspondingly, John Lennon's use of Rickenbackers boosted their sales to unprecedented levels.

The Beatles's first USA television broadcast was but the initial salvo in the so-called 'British Invasion'. Paradoxically, Harrison had chosen to play Gretsch because of his admiration for Chet Atkins, while Lennon purchased his first Rickenbacker (a Capri 325 model) in Hamburg, having seen Toots Thielemans playing a similar guitar with the George Shearing Quintet! Inevitably, Beatle clones began to appear, with their statutory Gretsches and Rickenbackers. Accordingly, retailers broadened their inventories to accommodate demand.

If the Beatles represented the cutting edge of popular music, the counterculture surrounding more obscure USA rhythm and blues (and blues) had become the *raison d'être* of the 'hip'. Neither were the Beatles totally removed from this culture. Before their almost exclusive concentration upon self-penned material, they too had drawn from similar obscure USA recordings, e.g. *You Really Got a Hold On Me* (Miracles), *Please Mr. Postman* (Marvelettes), *Money* (Barrett Strong) and, of course, *Roll Over Beethoven* (Chuck Berry). What the Beatles did for this latent American cult music, however, was to inadvertently open the doors for other British bands, such as the Animals, the Yardbirds, Them and perhaps most important of all, the Rolling Stones.

27. The Rolling Stones

While the Beatles's first American tour, in February 1964, was auspicious, the Rolling Stones followed them in June, further fuelling an American infatuation with British bands. The Stones were very forward in acknowledging their blues roots, paying homage to their idols, most of whom were black singer-guitarists from Chicago. Blues and R & B was then a minority interest in the States, which had been covertly suppressed in an attempt to prevent it reaching a young and predominantly white audience.

Important bluesmen, like Howlin' Wolf and Muddy Waters made guest appearances with the Rolling Stones, affording them overnight celebrity status. Whenever he was interviewed, the Stones's lead guitarist Keith Richards extolled the virtues of Chuck Berry, Jimmy Reed and Muddy Waters, thereby introducing many Americans to their own heritage. The Stones even made a pilgrimage to Chess Records, (the home of Chicago blues recordings) to record *Five by Five*, their first EP.

28. Eric Clapton

By the mid-1960s, rock and pop music had blossomed to a degree whereby the Rolling Stones were able to record a blues jam (*Goin' Home*) which lasted twelve minutes. Other blues-based groups also began to record marathon guitar solos, from the seminal *Blues Breakers -John Mayall with Eric Clapton* (1966) to Alvin Lee's epic guitar solos on *Ten Years After* (1967) and *Undead* (1968). The 'guitar hero' had arrived, encouraged in no small part by the apotheosis of Eric Clapton.

Blues Breakers - John Mayall with Eric Clapton (1966)

When in 1966 the graffiti on London walls proclaimed: 'Clapton is God', not only did the role of the electric guitarist change, but also the basic sound of the instrument. More explicitly blues-based than Keith Richards, Clapton had taken the playing style of Chuck Berry a stage further, as evidenced by his work on the *Five Live Yardbirds* album (1964). Synthesizing elements of his favorite blues guitarists, most notably Freddie and B. B. King, with his natural ability for phrasing and innate feel, Clapton wrote the 'handbook' for students of blues and blues-based rock. The raw, vital and distorted tone of his 1959 Gibson Les Paul, played at high volume through a 45 watt Marshall combo, was light years away from the electric guitar sounds of Bob Bogle and Hank Marvin.

With his deeply felt playing on the Blues Breakers album, Eric Clapton changed preconceptions regarding the sound of the electric guitar virtually overnight. The amplified guitar and distortion, to a lesser or greater degree, (depending upon the music), were now inextricably linked.

Those guitar heroes who followed Clapton, including Jimi Hendrix, Jeff Beck, and Mike Bloomfield, also used distortion-based sounds, caused either by overdriving their 'tube' amplifiers, or artificially generated by a sound processing foot pedal called a 'fuzz box'. This novel electric guitar sound coincided with the Beatles's influential experiments with sitars and electronic music (backward tape recordings, etc.) and marked a point in the development of the electric guitar when almost anything seemed possible.

29. The Age of Experiment

The experimental ethos of the time was reflected in the guitar merchandising industry, which spawned such oddities as Danelectro's 'Coral' brand electric sitars (1967-1970), the Vox Guitar Organ (1966-1967) and Rickenbacker's 336/12, convertible, a guitar which could be changed from 6 to 12 strings by means of a metal lever. Ominously, amplification was becoming larger and louder, and the sound processing 'effects units', like fuzz boxes and wah-wah pedals, began to appear. Not since the early experiments of Les Paul had electronics, per se, played such an influential role in the electric guitar's sound.

Bands like the Yardbirds, (with Clapton's replacement, Jeff Beck), the Rolling Stones, and the Spencer Davis Group had notable chart successes featuring distorted guitars, courtesy of the fuzz box, while Eric Clapton and Jimi Hendrix were early, and influential, advocates of the wah-wah pedals.

Despite these monumental advances in technology, the electric guitar in jazz was relatively late to adopt sound processing devices. Fusion players Larry Coryell (b.1943) and John McLaughlin (b.1942) were among the first, and arguably most adventurous electric guitarists in the jazz field to be involved with post-Clapton guitar sounds.

Though they still adhered doggedly to tradition, both jazz and country guitarists were nevertheless beginning to be influenced by contemporary 'pop' music. Wes Montgomery, Grant Green, Johnny Smith, Lenny Breau and George Benson, for example, recorded jazz versions of Beatles tunes, albeit with an undistorted pre-Claptonesque tone. Jazz giant Joe Pass recorded an entire album of Rolling Stones tunes in 1966, but given the harmonic limitations of the music, it was an ill-advised project which was not particularly successful.

Country music, too, was borrowing from pop, both in its repertoire (as evidenced by recordings like *Chet Atkins Picks On The Beatles)*, and in the unprecedented appearance of country/rock bands such as Area Code 601, the Flying Burrito Brothers, the Byrds and Buffalo Springfield. As had been the case with jazz, however, the fuzzy, overdriven, guitar sound was late in making an appearance. Indeed, the clean, bright tone favored by players such as Jimmy Bryant, Don Rich, and Roy Nichols, remains, to this day, a basic but vital ingredient of the country sound.

Much the same could be said of folk music. Bob Dylan's use of Mike Bloomfield's electric guitar on the 1965 recording *Highway 61 Revisited*, and at the Newport Folk Festival, was difficult for folk fans to stomach. Two years later folk-based groups, like the Lovin' Spoonful, the Band and, in England, Fairport Convention, Steeleye Span and Pentangle, were pumping out the volume on electric guitars, to the delight of diehard purists!

30. Jimi Hendrix

Until the spectacular emergence of Jimi Hendrix (1942-1970), in 1966, the electric guitar had been treated, essentially, as an amplified steel string, with artificially enhanced volume. Eric Clapton was largely responsible for making the overdriven amplifier an important aspect of the electric guitar's sound and, of course, various echo effects had been used since Les Paul's pioneering experiments during the 1940s.

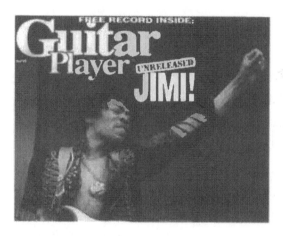

Jimi Hendrix featured on the cover of Guitar Player, May 1989

Until the appearance of Hendrix, however, no one had made the amplifier and primitive effects units of the day such an integral part of their music. Hendrix, it could be argued, played the amplifier as much as he played the guitar, harnessing the electronic potential of his 'instruments' as effectively and creatively as contemporary 'classical' composers like Karlheinz Stockhausen. His legendary rendition of *The Star-Spangled Banner*, performed during the Woodstock Festival of 1969, encompassed an eclectic elixir of rock, blues, avant- garde and free jazz.

67

Hendrix created an electric guitar soundscape uninhibited by what had gone before. He had travelled the long road from Chicago blues to an abstract world of treated sounds; *he* was the medium, his guitar the paintbrush and amplification the palette. Of all the electric guitarists to emerge during the 'Swingin' 60s', Jimi Hendrix remains the most influential.

31. The End of the 60s

As the 60s drew to a close, large powerful amplifiers and signal modifying effects units, had become the order of the day. Marathon guitar solos recorded by supergroup 'Cream', featuring Eric Clapton, were emblematic of guitar hero mania. Jeff Beck, Peter Green, Jimi Hendrix, Mike Bloomfield, Alvin Lee, Carlos Santana, Richie Blackmore, Jimmy Page and Gary Moore were among the guitarists who achieved cult status by the late 60s. Others were to follow, as the 70s witnessed greater harmonic sophistication and the blossoming of jazz-rock fusion.

By 1970, so many electric guitar idols had been and gone, that no one particular model or brand of electric guitar was in vogue. Clapton and Bloomfield popularized Les Pauls and were primarily responsible for Gibson's reintroduction of the model following a seven year hiatus in production.

Jimi Hendrix breathed new life into the Fender Stratocaster, blowing away its anachronistic associations with surf music and 'twee' instrumentals. Gretsch and Rickenbacker remained popular, but as the Beatles changed to Fenders, Gibsons and Epiphones so too did their fickle following. As in the previous decade, therefore, artistic associations ensured that Gibson and Fender remained the overall brand leaders.

PART VI: THE 1970s:
MATURITY - DIVERSITY

32. The Early 1970s

The cult of the guitar hero reached its height in the late 60s personified by the 1969 Woodstock Rock Festival in which such luminaries as Alvin Lee, Jimi Hendrix and Carlos Santana took guitar solos of epic proportions.

By the early 70s such self-indulgence had become passé. Blues forms had, for the most part, evolved into 'heavy metal', with the exception of a handful of purists whose music had, like modern jazz, become a minority interest.

Endless guitar solos, based on the twelve bar blues sequence, had become so commonplace that their spectator appeal had waned. Audiences and a growing number of musicians craved the greater sophistication of more progressive music, personified by fused styles. While the I, VI, V chord sequence of rock'n'roll would always retain a beloved place, the 1970s marked a new epoch in the harmonic development of popular music.

Concept albums from bands such as Yes, the Moodys, Pink Floyd and David Bowie helped fill the creative void previously occupied by virtuoso instrumentalists. At the same time, bands like Led Zeppelin, featuring the guitar of Jimmy Page, and the various reincarnations of the Jeff Beck group, kept one foot in the guitar hero camp. Such groups were not averse to drawing unashamedly upon their blues roots when the mood took them.

From necessity, guitar heroes, with blues or rock'n'roll backgrounds, began to explore new horizons. Richie Blackmore (b.1945), for example, turned to the classics in the band Deep Purple, hammering out heavy metal versions of such unlikely vehicles as Beethoven's Ninth (Choral) Symphony and even, from time to time, teaming up with full symphony orchestras (Concerto for Group and Orchestra).

Carlos Santana, John McLaughlin and Gary Moore flirted with jazz-rock fusion, but the really influential guitarists of the 1970s were the young studio players from the West Coast of America.

Larry Carlton (b.1948), Lee Ritenour (b.1952), Steve Lukather (b.1957) and Jay Graydon demonstrated a heightened form of sophistication, marrying slick jazz lines and subtle chording with the passion and soul of electric blues guitarists like B.B., Freddie and Albert King (not related). Their melodic string-bending showed literally thousands of guitarists that there was more to virtuoso guitar playing than power chords and minor pentatonic scales.

Paradoxically, these West Coast session players's choice of guitar, the Gibson ES335 seemed, at the time, quite anachronistic. It was perceived as the instrument of Chuck Berry and 1960s blues players like B.B. and Freddie King, Matt 'Guitar' Murphy, Earl Hooker and Magic Sam. Yet, the hollow, woody tone of Gibson's erstwhile semi-acoustic developed a snarling sustain when played at volume, a tone which gave the sinuous jazz lines of these young Americans a more contemporary rock'n'roll edge.

33. Larry Carlton and Lee Ritenour

Of the aforementioned players, Larry Carlton was probably the best known and almost certainly the most influential. By the mid-1970s he had gained prominence through his tasteful guitar work on albums by Joni Mitchell (*Hejira*), Steely Dan (*Aja*), Bobby Bland (*The Dreamer*), and jazz rock fusionists, the Crusaders (*Southern Comfort*). Carlton joined the Crusaders on a regular basis in 1975, and soon attained worldwide fame from recording and touring with these internationally recognized jazz instrumentalists. Carlton's rock and blues background provided a wonderful foil for their modern jazz style, creating a true synthesis which affected the musical concepts of both parties.

Larry Carlton in Guitar Player, May 1979

As the band grew more funky, Carlton's playing became more harmonically complex. The fact that he also retained the energy and excitement of his rock'n'roll roots, endowed his playing with an immediate and universal appeal. Record companies and promoters were quick to spot this and Larry Carlton's career, as the first of a new type of guitar hero, was affirmed by a series of albums including the eponymous *Larry Carlton* (1978), *Larry Carlton Strikes Twice* (1979) and *Mr 335 Live In Japan* (1979).

Lee Ritenour's style and popularity corresponded with Carlton's and the two were generally discussed in the same breath. As peers, they worked in the same Los Angeles recording studios, had similar musical backgrounds and used the same type of equipment, notably Gibson 335s and beefed-up Fenders or Mesa/Boogie amplifiers.

Lee Ritenour featured in Guitar, September 1979

Even their playing was strikingly similar in the idiomatic synthesis of blues and jazz. Both had previously played in rock bands, using Fender Stratocasters, and in jazz combos, with big-bodied Gibson archtops. Just as the Gibson 335 was a hybrid of the two, so were their musical concepts. Consequently the Gibson 335 became the very personification of these West Coast guitarists.

Broadly speaking, Ritenour demonstrated a little more jazz content, but his highly polished playing occasionally verged on the kind of smooth jazz frequently heard as background music. Carlton, on the other hand was, perhaps, marginally less polished, but commensurately more passionate, retaining something of the raw energy from his rock'n'roll days.

Superficially similar, Jay Graydon and Robben Ford also attained guitar celebrity status during the 1970s. Ford went on to make a name for himself as a harmonically adventurous blues player, while Graydon was unable to break away from the busy schedule of Los Angeles sessions and consequently, never obtained the full recognition his talents deserved.

34. Sophisticated Distortion

A major contributory factor to the smooth controlled sound produced by this group of West Coast session players, was the sophisticated management of distortion, via the careful alignment of two separate volume controls on their amplifiers.

During the early 70s, West Coast sound technicians, Paul Rivera and Randall Smith, began customizing small Fender, Princeton and Deluxe Reverb amplifiers. Besides beefing them up with larger transformers and higher output valves (tubes), the layout was also changed to incorporate a regular volume (or gain) which controlled the amount of natural distortion, and a master volume, which enabled the player to tap into the distortion at different levels and degrees of 'break-up'. This manipulation of distortion was much more sophisticated than any of the signal-processing effects units previously available, and led to a virtual revolution in the field of amplifier design.

Musicman, Peavey, Roland, Acoustic and, a little later, market leaders Fender began to produce guitar amplifiers based on this simple principle.

The most famous brand name to adopt this design, however, was Mesa/Boogie whose amplifiers were from the outset, closely associated with the influential West Coast players. For several years, the combination of a Gibson ES335 and a Mesa/Boogie Mark I or Mark II, became *the* industry standard for the marque of quality, sophistication and professionalism.

Larry Carlton playing a Gibson ES335 with Mesa/Boogie amplifier

At the other end of the spectrum, Jimmy Page's primal Les Paul Standard and Richie Blackmore's screaming Strat. were still being played through banks of high wattage Marshall amplification, exerting a powerful influence upon successive generations of excruciatingly loud heavy metal guitarists.

Nestling somewhere between these two extreme stylistic polarities were players like Carlos Santana, John McLaughlin and Jeff Beck, who approached jazz-rock fusion from a strong rock background, borrowing more heavily from Jimi Hendrix and Eastern cultures than from modern jazz per se. Despite a somewhat diluted commitment to the pure jazz tradition, these players nevertheless influenced the future direction of guitar playing in jazz, paving the way for later stylists such as John Scofield, Bill Frisell and Mike Stern.

35. John McLaughlin and Larry Coryell

John McLaughlin (b.1942) and Larry Coryell (b.1943) were among the first to mix elements of the jazz vocabulary (altered scales, chord substitutions, etc.) with the distorted tone and high volume of rock guitar. Between 1969 and 1972 both players made a significant impact on the direction of the guitar in modern jazz.

While their sound could be viewed as the antithesis of the fat, woody tone employed by Joe Pass, Barney Kessel, Jim Hall and Kenny Burrell, it was in actuality an extension, albeit radical, of their horn-like approach. By the mid-1970s feedback, sustain, fuzz and wah-wah had become commonplace in jazz, aided and abetted largely by trumpeter Miles Davis's classic recordings *In A Silent Way* (1969), *Bitches Brew* (1969), *Live-Evil* (1970) and *A Tribute To Jack Johnson* (1970), all of which featured a sonically uninhibited John McLaughlin.

McLaughlin and Coryell were eclectics, whose inquisitiveness resulted in a number of innovative experiments. Coryell flirted with the acoustic guitar and classical music, while McLaughlin made a huge impact, with the Mahavishnu Orchestra and (the acoustic), Shakti. Both groups were not only at the cutting edge of jazz-rock fusion, but also drew heavily from Asian music and Eastern philosophy.

McLaughlin went through a number of interesting guitars during the 1970s, from a solid-bodied Gibson double neck (six and twelve strings) to a unique Gibson acoustic with resonating, sympathetic strings which was based on the principle of the Indian sitar. He also played several instruments with scalloped fingerboards, which enabled him to make sitar-like string bends.

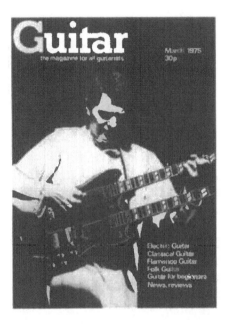

John McLaughlin in Guitar, March 1975

Several heavy metal players such as Richie Blackmore and, a decade later, Yngwie Malmsteen (b. 1963) also played guitars with scalloped fingerboards (Fender Stratocasters), in their search for greater string bending facility.

36. Jeff Beck and Eric Clapton in the 70s

Two of the most influential electric guitarists of the previous decade, Jeff Beck and Eric Clapton, reinvented themselves several times throughout the 1970s. Beck flirted with jazz-rock fusion, producing two classic albums: *Blow By Blow* (1975) and *Wired* (1976). His ability to get straight to the point musically, coupled with erstwhile Beatles producer George Martin's imaginative and sympathetic producing, resulted in two of the most important guitar records of the decade.

Eric Clapton, on the other hand, continued his paradoxical drift back towards the popular commerciality which he had previously cited as the reason for leaving the Yardbirds.

Eric Clapton on the cover of Strange Brew playing an early 60s Gibson ES335

Following a personality and name change the two disc set, *Derek and the Dominos* (1970), with Duane Allman, had a major hit with *Layla*. Yet, despite the success of this heartfelt song, Clapton had fallen prey to heroin addiction and spent much of the decade fighting personal demons. His albums *461 Ocean Boulevard* (1974) and *Slowhand* (1977), were particularly successful as were the singles *Wonderful Tonight* and *I Shot The Sheriff*, but it is debatable whether these works contributed much to the furtherance of the electric guitar. Clapton's main contribution, which was undoubtedly profound, lay in his earlier recordings with John Mayall's Bluesbreakers and Cream.

37. Summing up the 70s

Several iconoclastic figures emerged during the 70s, guitarists who had paid their dues during the previous decade, but failed to attract much in the way of critical acclaim. Alan Holdsworth (b.1948), Al Di Meola (b.1954), Robert Fripp (b.1946), Frank Zappa (1940-1993), Fred Frith (b.1949) and the tragically overlooked Ollie Halsall (1949-1992) took the electric guitar into previously uncharted territory.

While these players were individualists, each furrowing their own unique paths, a number of more readily accessible guitarists also appeared. Under the general umbrella of popular music (an increasingly expanding definition), guitarists Steve Howe (b.1947) with the band Yes, Andy Summers (b.1942) with Police and country-influenced Albert Lee, Emmylou Harris, the Crickets, the Everly Brothers, Eric Clapton, et al., all made their presence felt during the 1970s.

If the 1970s witnessed a good deal of diversification in popular music, much was superficial and short-lived. The theoretical glam rock and equally reactive, but diametrically opposed, punk movement were sucked unceremoniously into the mainstream. This jubilant escapism from the relative norm of the 60s had little effect upon the development of the electric guitar. Indeed, when Jimi Hendrix was found dead of a drugs overdose in 1970, the same year that the Beatles officially broke up and Peter Green began his descent into mental illness, things looked very bleak for the future of the electric guitar.

Fortunately, the 1970s also spawned several guitar-based rock bands such as the Eagles, whose *Hotel California* and *New Kid In Town*, featuring the twin guitars of Joe Walsh (b.1947) and Glen Frey (b.1948), were among the decade's classic recordings. Other important guitar-based bands to emerge in the 70s included Queen, featuring Brian May (b.1947), Police, with Andy Summers and Dire Straits, with the Shadows-influenced Strat. of Mark Knopfler (b.1949).

In broad terms, the electric guitar was becoming less relevant in popular music, with a general swing towards keyboards and electronics. Paradoxically, it was evident by the late 70s, that the punk subculture had become increasingly dependent on the high energy, primal, guitar sounds which had characterized authentic rock'n'roll and the early 60s British R & B movement.

Neither were the 1970s a time of significant advances in guitar technology. There was a continued preoccupation with sustain, which led to the introduction of heavy-duty brass fittings (nuts, bridges, tailpieces, etc.), and a general trend towards heavier instruments. Travis Bean and Kramer built guitars with aluminium necks and a number of handmade instruments (John Birch, Zematis, Alembic, et al.) gained a foothold in an increasingly fickle market.

The 70s also witnessed a growth in 'aftermarket' replacement parts, such as pickups (Dimarzio, Bill Lawrence, Schaller) and tuning pegs (Schaller, Grover, Gotah) as well as early, but relatively crude, attempts at electronic synthesis.

PART VII: THE TURBULENT YEARS

38. Development and Turbulence

If the 1970s proved stylistically eclectic, a number of trends promulgated during that confused decade were, nevertheless, further developed in the 80s. Two specific areas, namely the crude sonic and anarchic sounds of punk and the diametrically opposed 'retro-movement', (with its attention to detail and preoccupation with mimicking a bygone age), proved central to the electric guitar during the 80s. In many respects this was its most turbulent decade. What pop historians refer to as the 'post modern period' saw the growth of counter-cultures like house music and its spin-offs, rap and hip-hop. If rock'n'roll was inextricably associated with the electric guitar, house music was essentially the result of affordable synthesizers, sequencers, samplers and drum machines.

Sequencers allowed musicians to store musical sequences and to then play them back through synthesizers, while samplers could sample any recorded sound and mix them together with the synthesized material. A new era of music technology developed at an alarming rate. For a time, at least, the electric guitar was practically overshadowed, viewed either as an anachronism, or as the tool of egocentric posers.

Running parallel to this technological evolution was a variety of trends. The 'new romantics', for example, were a movement based on the more theatrical aspects of 70s glam rock as well as being a knee jerk reaction to the perceived sterility of electronic music. There was also a renewed interest in the music and instruments of the late 50s and early 60s, which manifested itself in an amazing stream of reissue guitars and amplifiers, together with a regeneration of basic blues and rock'n'roll music.

80

Guitars from the 1970s and early 80s tended to suffer from an inconsistency of quality. The larger manufacturers, in particular, grew so concerned with cost cutting that, over a period of time, their instruments changed dramatically. These were not always particularly well received and as a consequence guitarists turned to the increasing number of high quality Japanese instruments (by such companies as Ibanez, Yamaha and Tokai) or sought out Vintage guitars from the 50s and 60s.

Specialist Vintage stores, like Gruhn's of Nashville, Mandolin Brothers (Statten Island), Guitar Trader (New York) and Norm's Rare Guitars (Los Angeles), sprang up to meet this growing demand, while Gibson and Fender set about reissuing tried and tested models from the past.

Fender US Vintage Reissue (from the Fender Catalog)

Gibson Les Pauls and 335s (together with Fender Telecasters and Stratocasters), following the specifications of their illustrious predecessors, were also foremost in their eagerness to recreate the glory days of the electric guitar. The big companies had, of course, previously dabbled with the retrospective, reissue market. Gibson's reintroduction of the original Les Paul model in 1968 was an early indication of things to come. A commitment to total accuracy, however, had to wait until the 1980s, although the 1954 Les Paul Custom reissue (1972/3) had been a notable attempt at capturing the true essence of a vintage guitar.

Gibson's Heritage 80, and Heritage 80 Elite Les Paul Standards, the subsequent 1959 Les Paul Standard and ES335 dot neck reissues, all re-appeared during the early 80s, marking a trend which would soon be followed by most other major companies.

Fender reissued their 1952 Telecaster, together with 1957 and 1962 Stratocasters in 1982, closely followed by imitations of other popular models (Jazzmaster, Jaguar, Thinline and Rosewood Teles, etc.) many of which were actually manufactured in Japan. Rickenbacker's 'Vintage Series' first appeared in 1984, with a plethora of models closely associated with 60s bands like the Beatles, the Byrds, the Who and Steppenwolf.

Noting this retrospective trend, amplifier companies also re-examined their product. Marshall, for example, reissued their 45 watt 'Bluesbreaker' combo, which had been partly responsible for Clapton's iconoclastic tone on the Blues Breakers album (1966), while Vox once again revamped its eponymous AC30, bringing the model a little closer to the 1960s specifications, in which format it had made a significant contribution to the British beat boom. Fender, on the other hand, were surprisingly slow to get their reissue amplifiers on the roster, although they did hire Paul Rivera to revamp their existing range of tube amplifiers which were, coincidentally, given the same 'black faced' cosmetics of the early 60s models.

With this growing trend towards retro gear, came a renewed interest in the roots of popular guitar music, especially blues and 1950s rock'n'roll. Stevie Ray Vaughan (1954-1990) must be seen as the catalyst for a 1980s blues revival, which closely echoed a similar trend some twenty years earlier. Blues guitarists like Stevie and his brother Jimmie, Gary Moore, Bonnie Raitt and Robben Ford initiated a revival which, in turn, promoted the work of B. B. King, Albert King (1923-99), Albert Collins (1932-93) and John Lee Hooker (b.1917). Yet similarities with the 1960s were to prove tenuous, for whereas the 60s blues boom fizzled out after four or five years, the effects of the 80s revival remain with us today, albeit in a diluted form. Stevie Ray Vaughan's first significant appearance came in 1983 on David Bowie's *Let's Dance*. His album, *Texas Flood* (1983), inspired a generation of young guitarists to buy themselves Sunburst Fender Stratocasters, and even copies of Vaughan's 'signature' cowboy hat!

Sadly, Stevie Ray Vaughan was killed in a plane crash in 1990, just as he was about to begin a tour with Eric Clapton, exposure which would, almost certainly, have won him a much larger audience. Fender paid tribute to this influential guitarist by issuing a Stevie Ray Vaughan 'signature' Stratocaster (1992), a replica of the guitar he had used for over two decades.

39. Some Significant Blues Players

Noting the growing blues revival, Fender also issued 'signature' guitars for three other significant blues players, Albert Collins, Bonnie Raitt and Buddy Guy.

Albert Collins (1932-93) had been a popular R & B artist since the success of his instrumental *Frosty* in the early 60s. Working the tedious routine of bars, roadhouses and the Chitlin Circuit, Collins seemed unable to reach a wider audience. Even his brief, but limited, success at the tail end of the 1960s blues boom, did little to lift him from obscurity.

But a series of recordings for the Alligator record label during the 1980s finally furnished the opportunity he deserved, providing him with blues superstar status comparable to B. B. King, Buddy Guy and John Lee Hooker.

Albert Collins pictured on his 'Complete Imperial Recordings' publication

Collins had a trebly, aggressive sound, the coldness of which earned him the appropriate nickname of the Iceman. Influenced by the Hammond organ, double-stops, pedal notes and D minor tuning set Collins apart from his contemporaries. So too did his customized Telecaster, a replica of which was issued by the Fender Custom Shop in 1990.

Many of the 80s bluesmen obtained greater exposure through their mentors. Buddy Guy, for example, benefitted from his association with Eric Clapton, and John Lee Hooker could be found either touring or recording with Van Morrison. This 'white boy' helps 'black blues musician' scenario mirrored earlier activities of bands like the Rolling Stones, John Mayall's Bluesbreakers and Alexis Korner's Blues Incorporated.

While it is heartening to witness this active support, it is viewed, in some quarters, as being the entirely appropriate action for 'stealing' their music in the first place! (White guitarists, accused of such plagiarism, include Eric Clapton and Bonnie Raitt, both of whom, like their blues heroes, also had 'signature' Stratocasters issued by Fender during the late 80s and early 90s.)

40. The New Age Jazz

If the earthy, honest tones of Albert Collins, Buddy Guy and John Lee Hooker harked back to the elemental guitar sounds of the 1960s, there were those at the opposite end of the spectrum whose experiments with synthesis and electronic technologies also proved influential. Pat Metheny (b.1954), Bill Frisell (b.1951), Alan Holdsworth (b.1948), Robert Fripp (b.1946), and Adrian Belew (b.1951), were all playing 'genre busting' music during the 80s.

While much of their music defies definition, it could perhaps best be loosely described as New Age Jazz. Of the five aforementioned players, Metheny remained the most traditional, having been influenced heavily by Jim Hall and Wes Montgomery. Frisell was the most eclectic, whilst Fripp, Belew and Holdsworth were, and remain to this day, the most overtly experimental.

Adrian Belew featured in Guitar Player, January 1984

What they did have in common, however, was the search for different sounds which led to experiments with the then newly developed Synth-Axe (Holdsworth, Metheny, Belew, Frisell). Fripp's fascination with electronics resulted in *Frippertronics*, an interface with guitar and tape-repeat effects which was, in essence, a marriage of Les Paul and Karlheinz Stockhausen (b.1928).

41. Pat Metheny

Pat Metheny was arguably the most musically accessible, which would account for his wide popularity, attracting an even larger audience when he teamed up with singer/songwriter Joni Mitchell. (Apart from their cult status among other musicians and a small but discerning audience, Holdsworth, Belew and Fripp remained less than household names.)

Pat Metheny in Guitar Player, December 1981

His signature sound, produced by a Gibson ES175, treated with copious amounts of chorus and delay, was widely copied by other jazz guitarists. Even such individualists as John Scofield (b.1951), and Mike Stern (b.1953), were seduced by this beguiling sound, though it proved anathema to lovers of the unprocessed and organic distorted tones usually associated with the electric guitar.

John Scofield featured in Downbeat, January 1987

42. Grunge

No examination of the electric guitar in the 1980s would be complete without reference to 'Grunge'. This was a legacy of the primitive playing style which emerged during the Punk movement, a style in which noise and energy were emphasized at the expense of technique and finesse. Grunge also drew from the repetitive riffing style of Heavy Metal, although its music was generally more bombastic and multi-textured. Kurt Cobain (1967-94) was among the first to prove that a guitarist had no need to be articulately gifted, fast, or harmonically knowledgeable to create vital sounds.

Using cheap junk shop guitars, players like Stone Gossard (b.1966), Mike McCready (b.1965) and Thurston Moore arrived at unconventional tunings and prepared instruments (similar to John Cage's prepared pianos), in order to create huge textured soundscapes which were diametrically opposed to the self-indulgent virtuosic displays of the 'guitar hero'.

43. Shred

Despite being hugely out of fashion, the guitar hero syndrome was nevertheless perpetuated by a group of metal/blues influenced guitarists. Foremost among these was Eddie Van Halen (b.1957), whose two-handed tapping style was soon adopted by dozens of would-be guitar virtuosos. Joe Satriani (b.1956), Yngwie Malmsteen (b.1963) and Steve Vai (b.1960) also built their styles around the concept of Paganini-like virtuosity, a blatantly extrovert approach appropriately called 'Shred'.

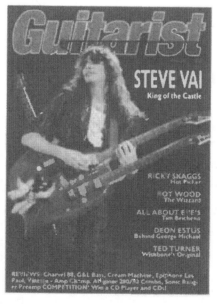

Steve Vai in Guitar Player, November 1988

Shred involved excessive speed and volume, together with the concomitant face-pulling of a tortured soul! While such playing was important in once again raising the technical possibilities of the instrument, Shred eventually resulted in a backlash.

44. Consolidation

By the 90s, players and listeners alike had, by and large, forsaken the excesses of virtuosity for a style of guitar music with more feeling. Eric Clapton and Jeff Beck retained their positions as high priests of the electric guitar, while other long-established players such as John McLaughlin, Larry Carlton, Robben Ford, Lee Ritenour, Roy Buchanan (1939-88) and James Burton (b. 1939) continued to make valuable contributions to the electric guitar pantheon. Other guitarists whose high quality playing made a strong impression during the 80s include Danny Gatton (1945-94) and Eric Johnson (b.1954).

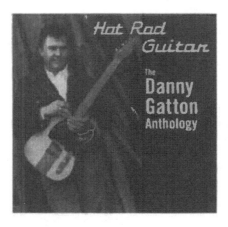

Danny Gatton - Anthology on Rhino RS 75691

If the electric guitar did manage to keep a presence throughout the 80s, the decade was not particularly memorable for innovation. The instrument's position, both as a cross-cultural icon and a serious solo voice, was certainly affirmed.

Joe Pass and Stanley Jordan (b.1959) built on the former work of fingerstyle virtuoso, Lenny Breau (1941-1984), taking the solo electric guitar to a new level, while establishing and popularizing the concept of unaccompanied electric guitar through television recordings and pseudo classical concerts.

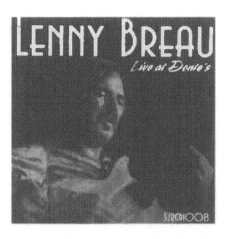

Lenny Breau plays (on String Jazz SJRCD1008)

Joe Pass's remarkable series of 'Virtuoso' recordings, for Norman Granz's Pablo label, stand as milestones in the instrument's development and are now the accepted benchmark for solo guitar playing.

Stanley Jordan's novel approach of two-handed tapping had its roots in the work of Jimmy Webster, a 1950s and 60s demonstrator for Gretsch guitars. Jordan took the concept much further, improvising complex jazz solos and multi-textured counterpoint.

Despite a precocious talent, Stanley Jordan's use of ultra-light gauge strings and a solid-bodied Travis Bean guitar with an aluminium neck, together with the absence of sustain inherent in the tapping technique, resulted in a rather bland, cool tone. Put more simply, he was a guitarist's guitarist whose playing, whilst visually spectacular, has somehow failed, as yet, to make a lasting impression on the public at large.

Predictably, advances in technology, during the 80s, were predominantly confined to electronics. It was paradoxical that at the very time amplifier companies were striving to recapture former glories by returning to basics, a revolution in digitized rack-mountable equipment was under way. For a period, digitally processed, delay, chorus distortion and echo units virtually rendered the basic combo (amplifier and speaker together in one unit), obsolete. Improvements in printed circuitry resulted in a tremendous growth in the market of add-on sound processors. Amplifiers generally became lighter, louder and, for the most part, smaller. Die-hard rockers and blues players tended to stay with the more conventional Marshall stacks, or tube combos, their maxim: the bigger they are the louder they are!

Refinements to the electric guitar were also limited to electronics, principally by improvements in the tracking of guitar synthesizers, and the introduction of more powerful, electronically active guitar pickups.

PART VIII: THE NEW MILLENNIUM

45. Problems of Definition

The electric guitar has always given rise to problems of definition, and no more so than as we move into the new millennium. From the 30s to the 70s things were relatively simple, for the electric guitar clearly meant the EADGBE tuned Spanish guitar made louder with the aid of an electronic sound system.

Problems of definition lay in the nature of the music, or musics, it was applied to. The Spanish guitar, with nylon strings, had no such problem of identity because its applications seldom veer far from its classical roots.

There is no such correlation between the electric guitar and its music. The playing of Wes Montgomery and Jimi Hendrix, Hank Marvin and Thurston Moore, Albert Lee and Kurt Cobain are typical examples of diametrically opposed musics emanating from essentially the same instrument. Unlike the classical guitar, the electric instrument has no real pedigree - the electric guitar, played exclusively with the plectrum, and with no sound processing whatsoever, had its last great exponent in Johnny Smith. (Smith has not performed in public since the 1970s, and while some of his 1950s recordings have been reissued on compact disc, his last recording, *Legends,* released in 1994 was actually made in 1976.)

Because the electric guitar means so many different things to different people, it is impossible to predict its future with any degree of accuracy. One encouraging development is the fact that the electric guitar, albeit under a general definition, is now being taught in a number of music colleges and conservatories.

Lack of concensus about what the electric guitar actually is and does, however, had militated against the growth of reliable pedagogy. As one would expect, given the instrument's stylistic parameters, the best books, videos and other teaching aids are those which relate narrowly, and quite specifically, to aspects of a single style such as jazz or country.

Not only is the music associated with the electric guitar multifaceted, so too are the styles and fashions which ultimately define its identity. While such pluralities have ensured its longevity, they have also weakened the case for its position as a serious musical instrument equivalent in status to those in symphony orchestras, military and even dance bands. Yet, the electric guitar remains the instrument of the people and therein lies its strength. Until fashions change dramatically the electric guitar will retain a foothold, and there are enough interested minorities to guarantee a significant number of guitar-related revivals. The electric guitar is here to stay.

Perhaps, without its multifarious background, the electric guitar would not have become the 20th century icon it did. In this new millennium, the instrument is both old enough to represent nostalgic symbolism and young enough to convey the rebelliousness of youth cultures. Indeed, the 1980s and 90s saw the continuation of the electric guitar being used to vent the pent-up aggression of disenchanted youth as evidenced in the sonic barrages of groups like Nirvana, the Smashing Pumpkins and Sonic Youth.

At the same time, guitarists like Jimmy Bruno and Howard Alden appear to have been continuing the more traditional approach of Johnny Smith, Barney Kessel and George Van Eps. This almost anachronistic regression to a purer electric guitar sound and conventional plectrum technique, proved a striking characteristic of the 90s. And, while we are not talking about any more than a dozen or so prominent practitioners, interest in the pre-1960s history of the electric guitar seems to be on the increase. Reissues of classic recordings by such important figures as Tal Farlow, Johnny Smith, Jimmy Bryant, Merle Travis, et al., are, it would appear, having an effect upon contemporary players. How tangible this influence will be, remains to be seen.

46. Replicas

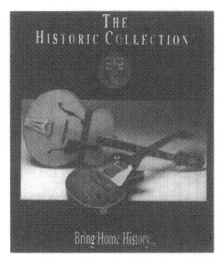

The Gibson Historic Collection Catalog

In the early years of the new millennium, the practice of producing replicas of vintage guitars is gathering momentum. Fender's Custom Shop, in Corona, California has even developed the techniques of 'distress' finishes and corroded hardware to create the authentic vintage appearance. (Gibson also apply similar 'distressing' processes to selected models in their Historic Series of reissues.)

Fender's Time Machine series of vintage reissue Stratocasters and Telecasters falls into three distinct categories:

1. *N.O.S. (New Old Stock)* as if the guitar was bought new in its respective year and brought forward in time to the present day.

2. *Closet Classic* as if the guitar was bought new in its respective year, played perhaps a dozen times a year and then put carefully away. Has a few small 'dings', lightly checked finish, oxidized hardware and aged plastic parts.

3. *Relic* shows natural wear and tear of years of heavy use, nicks, scratches, worn finish, rusty hardware and aged plastic parts.

(Fender Frontline Catalog, pp. 122/125, Volume 26, July/December, 1999, Fender Publications)

As one might expect, such instruments, which are essentially replicas, have met with a mixed reception, although most agree that they play and sound remarkably well.

47. The Parker Fly

The most radical new development in recent times has been the Parker 'Fly'. The aptly titled Fly, designed by Ken Parker in the early 90s, was probably the most innovative electric guitar in over two decades. Essentially based upon the solid-body guitar, its softwood body, coated with a thin layer of plastic, is both durable and remarkably light; weighing in at 6 pounds or less, the Fly represents the very antithesis of the heavyweight instruments which were so popular during the 70s and 80s.

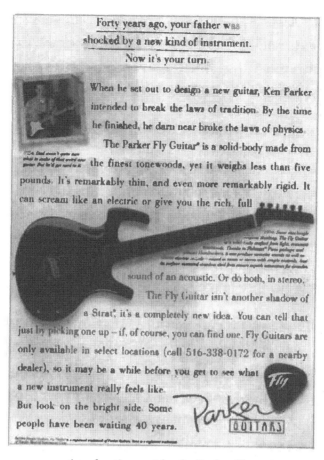

An advertisement for the Parker Fly

A good deal of time and computer dimensioning was spent on the Parker Fly's ergonomic design in the quest for increased comfort and lightness. This also resulted in a futuristic shape, a development which mirrored the introduction of the Fender Stratocaster way back in 1954. Besides its unusual shape and remarkably light weight, the fingerboard of the Fly is made of carbon fiber, fitted with heavy steel frets, designed to provide years of wear-free use.

Due to the success and popularity of more traditional guitars like the Gibson Les Paul and 335, and Fender's Stratocaster and Telecaster, the Parker Fly initially met with consumer resistance. But in the hands of players such as Pat Martino, and Vernon Reid its future looks bright.

48. Further Developments in Amplification

Developments in amplification continue to follow the trends established during the 1980s. Hi-tech, rack-mounted effects remain popular, as do the retro-based reissue combos and large powerful stacks favored by heavy metal bands. At the same time, there is an increasing market in so-called 'designer' or 'boutique' amplifiers. These are expensive, hand-wired units, using the highest quality components.

Generally finished with eye-catching cosmetics, such as pink or blue vinyl covering, and highly polished chrome hardware, such amplifiers sell at a premium. Most are relatively low-tech, utilizing circuitry and old-fashioned Alnico magnet speakers. Indeed, much of their appeal is based on the supercilious retro movement, the motto of which appears to be: 'They don't make them like they used to!'

The obverse of this niche for high-end custom equipment is the abundance of cheap, serviceable products. It is far easier nowadays to purchase budget instruments which are actually playable, stay in tune and sound well. This was certainly not the case fifty years ago, when the majority of budget instruments were only fit to hang on the wall. The same applies to amplifiers. Thus it is relatively easy for the budding electric guitarist to get started.

49. Looking Forward

Who knows what the 21st century could bring? The electric guitar, starting from a powerful vantage point, has paid its dues and continues to consolidate its position of strength in a variety of musical genres.

The Electric Guitar: A Chronology of Evolution

1920:   L. Loar and L. A. Williams build prototype L4s with electrostatic pickups.

1932:   George Beauchamp, Paul Barth and Adolph Rickenbacker produce the 'Fry Pan' electric guitar.

1935:   Gibson develops the electric lap steel EH150.

1936:   Gibson markets the first 'practical' electric guitar: the ES150 (Charlie Christian) model.

1937:   Epiphone, Kay, National and Vega begin manufacturing electric guitars.

1938/39:   Slingerland's style 401, Electric Spanish Guitar represents the first serious solid- body electric guitar.

1941:   Les Paul experiments with the 'Log', the precursor to all semi-acoustic guitars and catalyst for the Les Paul solid-body guitar.

1943:   DeArmond manufactures a clip-on electro-magnetic pickup for archtop guitars.

1945:   Doc Kauffman and Leo Fender begin manufacturing lap steels.

1948:   Paul Bigsby and Merle Travis design and promote a solid-body electric guitar utilizing many features later found on Fenders and Gibsons.

1949/50:   Fender design and manufacture the 'Broadcaster', later called the No-Caster and Telecaster. Gibson introduces an entire range of new electric guitars, together with a pickup-pickguard attachment to electrify acoustic models.

1952:   Gibson introduces its first solid-body electric - the Les Paul (goldtop).

1953:   Rickenbacker recruits Roger Rossmeisl and starts manufacturing a range of solid-body electrics.

1954:   Fender Stratocaster launched. Gretsch enters the solid-body electric market. Gibson adds another solid-body (Les Paul Custom) to its range.

1955:   National, Kay, Harmony, etc., begin manufacturing solid-body electrics.

1956:   Seth Lover invents the 'humbucking' pickup, soon to be fitted on all but the lowest price Gibsons.

1957:   Fender broadens its range with the Jazzmaster and electric mandolins.

1958:   Gibson introduces the Les Paul Standard Flametop, together with the ES335 range of semi-acoustics and several other solid-bodied guitars.

1960:   Les Paul model redesigned in a double cutaway shape (renamed SG in 1961). Single cutaway Les Paul discontinued. Vox AC30 (twin) introduced.

1964:   Rickenbacker 3302/12 introduced (not the first, but the most popular 12 string guitar).

1965:   Vox Guitar Organ appears - with the most technologically advanced electrics until guitar synthesizers.

1967:   The Coral electric sitar launched - played as a guitar but producing pseudo sitar sounds.

1968:   Single cutaway Les Paul (custom and standard) reintroduced by popular demand.

1969:   Ampeg/Dan Armstrong manufacture perspex (see-through) guitars.

1972:   Gibson reissues 1954 Les Paul Custom.

1974:   Travis Bean introduces solid guitars with aluminium necks. Gibson reissues Les Paul Special.

1976:   Kramer guitar company founded, initially making solid guitars with aluminium necks, with wooden inserts.

1980:   Gibson reissues late 50s ES335 dot neck. Les Paul Heritage 80 introduced with specifications closer to the 1958/60 model.Roland introduces G202, 303, 505 and 808 guitar synthesizers.

1981:   Steinberger introduces headless guitars, made from a carbon graphite composite material.

1982:   Fender reissues 1952 Telecaster and 1957 and 62 Stratocasters. Steinberger bought out by Gibson, but continues to make carbon graphite/composite, headless, guitars.

1984:   Rickenbacker launch their series of vintage reissues. British company introduces Synthaxe. Roland introduces G707 and G77 guitar and bass synthesizer controllers.

1986:   Ibanez X-ING MIDI electronic guitar system and Stepp DGI introduced.

1987:   Casio introduces digital guitar (DG20).

1988:   Casio introduces self-contained PG380 guitar synthesizer.

1989:   Roland introduce the GK2 synthesizer driver.

1992:   The lightweight futuristic, Parker Fly, introduced in an attempt to produce a contemporary classic.

1993:   Gibson launches 'Historic'collection of replica vintage guitars.

1994:   Fender launches 'relic' series of distressed-finish Stratocaster and Telecaster vintage reissues.

1998:   Fender broadens its range of 'aged' vintage reissues - 'The Time Machine Series'.

Select Bibliography

Alexander, C. ed, *Masters of the Jazz Guitar: The Story of the Players and their Music,* Balafon, 1999.

Bacon, T. and Day, P.; *The Ultimate Guitar Book.* Dorling Kindersley, 1991.
The Fender Book. Balafon/IMP, 1992.
The Gibson Les Paul Book. Balafon/IMP, 1993.
The Rickenbacker Book. Balafon/IMP, 1994.
The Gretsch Book. Balafon/IMP, 1996.

Bellson, J. *The Gibson Story.* Gibson, 1973.

Bishop, I. *The Gibson Guitar from 1950.* Vols 1 &2. Musical New Services,1977.

Broadbent, P. *Charlie Christian - The Seminal Electric Guitarist.* Ashley Mark, 1997.

Carter, W. *Gibson Guitars, 100 Years of an American Icon.* General Publishing, 1994.

Carter, W. *Epiphone, The Complete History.* Hal Leonard, 1995.

Charlesworth, C. *A-Z of Rock Guitarists.* Proteus, 1982.

Da Pra, V. *Sunburst Alley (A Pictorial Gallery of the Les Paul Sunburst 1958-60).* Centerstream/Hal Leonard, 1997.

Duchossoir, A.R. *Gibson Electrics,* Vol. 1. Mediapresse, 1981.
Guitar Identification: Fender, Gibson, Gretsch, Martin. Mediapresse, 1983.
The Fender Telecaster. Hal Leonard, 1991
The Fender Stratocaster (40th Anniversary Edition). Hal Leonard, 1994.
Gibson Electrics - The Classic Years. Hal Leonard, 1994.

Evans, T., and M. A. *Guitars from Renaissance to Rock.* Paddington Press, 1977.

Fisch, J. and Fred, L. B. *Epiphone - The House of Stathopoulo.* Amsco, 1996.

Fleigler, R. *Amps: The Other Half of Rock'n'Roll.* Centerstream/Hal Leonard, 1993.

Giltrap, G. and Marten, N. *The Hofner Guitar - A History.* Music Maker, 1993.

Gregory, H. *1000 Great Guitarists.* Balafon, 1994.

Gruhn, G. and Carter, W. *Guide to Vintage Guitars.* GPI/Miller Freeman, 1991.
Electric Guitars and Basses. GPI,1994.

Howe, S. *The Steve Howe Guitar Collection.* Balafon, 1994.

Ingram, A. *Wes Montgomery.* Ashley Mark, 1985.
The Gibson ES175 - Its History and Players. Music Maker,1994.
The Gibson L5 - Its History and Players. Centerstream/Hal Leonard, 1997.

Kozinn, A., Welding P., Forte, D., Santoro, G. *The Guitar, The History, The Music, The Players,* Columbus/Quarto, 1984.

Moust, H. *The Guild Guitar Book.* Guitarchives/Hal Leonard, 1995.

Peterson, D. and Denney, D. *The Vox Story.* Bold Strummer, 1993.

Prown, P. and Newquist, H. *Legends of Rock Guitar.* Hal Leonard, 1997.

Sallis, J., ed. *The Guitar in Jazz: An Anthology.* University of Nebraska, 1996.

Schmidt, P. W. *Acquired of the Angels: The Lives and Works of Master Guitar Makers John D'Angelico and James D'Aquisto.* Scarecrow Press, 1990.

Scott, J. *The Guitars of the Fred Gretsch Company.* Centerstream/Hal Leonard, 1992.

Seguret, C. *The World of Guitars.* Greenwich Editions, 1999.

Shaw, R. *Great Guitars.* Hugh Lauter Levin Associates, 1997.

Smith, R. *The Complete Story of Rickenbacker Guitars.* Centerstream/Hal Leonard, 1987.

Smith, R. *Fender - The Sound Heard Round the World.* Garfish Pub./Music Sales, 1995.

Summerfield, M. J. *The Jazz Guitar: Its Evolution, Its Players and Personalities Since 1900* (4th Edition). Ashley Mark, 1998.

Trynka, P., ed. *The Electric Guitar, An Illustrated History.* Chronicle Books, 1995.

Van Hoose, T. *The Gibson Super 400 - Art of the Fine Guitar.* GPI Books/Miller Freeman, 1991.

Wheeler., T. *American Guitars.* Harper & Row, 1982.

Recommended Listening

Pioneers

George Barnes - *George Barnes and his Octet* - Hindsight HRS 106

Charlie Christian - *Charlie Christian, Genius of Electric Guitar* - Sony SNY 40846

Charlie Christian - *Live Session at Mintons* DMA JAZZ DM 15001

Tiny Grimes - *The Complete 1944-1950* - Blue Moon BMCD 6005

Lonnie Johnson - *Steppin On The Blues* - Roots'N'Blues 467252-2

Lonnie Johnson - *He's A Jelly Roll Baker* - Bluebird 07863 66064-2

Eddie Lang/Lonnie Johnson - *Blue Guitars,* Vols I and II - B G O BGOCD327

Oscar Moore - *1940 Era* - Tampa TP22

Les Paul - *The Complete Trios (1936-47)* - Decca/MCA MCAD - 11708

Les Paul - *Les Paul Trio* - LL 15741

Les Paul - *Les Paul's Country Roots* - BRON 9023

Floyd Smith - *Relaxin' with Floyd* - BB8752 - Black + Blue

Various - *Pioneers of Jazz Guitar* - Yazoo YAZ 1057

T-Bone Walker - *The Complete Capitol/Black and White Sessions* - Capitol Blues Collection 7243 8 29379 2 0

T-Bone Walker - *Inventor Of the Electric Guitar Blues* - Blues Boy RBD 304

T-Bone Walker - *The Beginning 1929-1946* - EPM Blues Collection 158852

The Jazz Age

Tal Farlow - *This is Tal Farlow* - Verve 537746

Barney Kessel - *The Pollwinners* - Contemporary OJC 156

Barney Kessel - *Barney Kessel Plays Standards* - Contemporary OJC 238

Mundell Lowe - *Mundell Lowe Quartet* - Riverside RLP204

Red Norvo Trio (with Tal Farlow) - *Move* - Savoy SV-0168

Les Paul - *Best of the Capitol Masters* - CAP 996 7

Jimmy Raney - *Jimmy Raney Visits Paris* - Fresh Sounds CD89

Jimmy Raney - *Tres Chouette* - VOGUE VG 651

Sal Salvador - *Quintet/Quartet* - Blue Note 7234-4-9654822

Johnny Smith - *Johnny Smith and His New Quartet* - Fresh Sounds FSR-CD80

Johnny Smith - *Moonlight in Vermont* - CAP 97747

Various - *The Great Guitars of Tal Farlow, Sal Salvador and Lou Mecca* - Blue Note CJ285127

Speedy West and Jimmy Bryant - *2 Guitars Country Style* - Capitol 1550831

Rock'n'Roll

Chet Atkins - *Guitar Genius* - RCA 753

Chet Atkins - *The Essential* - RCA 66855

Chuck Berry - Any early Chess recordings or Greatest Hits Compilation

Johnny Burnette - *Rock'n'Roll/Tear it Up* - B G O BGOCD177

Eddie Cochran - *Somethin' Else (Compilation)* - Razor & Tie RE 2162-2

Duane Eddy - *$1,000,000.00 Worth of Twang* - Jamie

Duane Eddy - *Twang Thang* - Rhino, RHIN 71223

Bill Haley - *Bill Haley - The E P Collection* - See for Miles Records Ltd SEECD 378

Dale Hawkins - *OH! Suzy* - Q - MCA MCD 30693

Buddy Holly - *Buddy Holly - From The Original Master Tapes* - MCA MCAD 5540

Elvis Presley - *Elvis Presley - The Sun Collection* - RCA ND 890106

Tommy Steele - *The Rock'n'Roll Years* - See for Miles Records Ltd SEE CD 203

Various - *Best Rock'n'Roll Album in the World - Ever!* - Virgin VTDCD 37

Gene Vincent - *Bluejean Bop!* - Magic Records 4975732

The Swingin'60s

Chet Atkins - *Down Home* - RCA Camden LPM 2350

The Beatles - *With the Beatles* - Parlophone CDP 7464362

The Beatles - *Sgt. Pepper's Lonely Hearts Club Band* - Parlophone - CDP 7461422

Jeff Beck - *Truth and Bec-ola* - EMI CDP 7954692

Chuck Berry - *The EP Collection* - See for Miles Records Ltd SEE CD 320

Kenny Burrell - *Guitar Forms* - Verve 521403

Cream - *Disraeli Gears* - Polydor 8236362

Hank Garland - *Jazz Winds From a New Direction* - Columbia 4925322

Jimi Hendrix - *Are You Experienced ?*- MCA MCD 11608

B. B. King - *Live At the Regal* - BGO Records BGOCD235

Freddy King - *Just Pickin'* - Modern Blues MBXLCD-721

The Kinks - *EP Collection* - See For Miles Records Ltd SEE CD 295

John Mayall/Eric Clapton - *Blues Breakers/John Mayall with Eric Clapton* - Deram 844 827-2

John McLaughlin - *Extrapolation* - Polydor 849 069

Wes Montgomery - *The Incredible Jazz Guitar Of* - Riverside OJCD - 036-2

Wes Montgomery - *Movin' Wes* - Verve 521 433-2

Joe Pass - *Joy Spring* - Pacific Jazz CDP 8352222

The Rolling Stones- *Aftermath* - London 8445662

The Rolling Stones - *12 x 5* - London 8444612

The Shadows - *The Shadows* - EMI 7243-4 98937 2 6

The Shadows - *Out of the Shadows* - EMI 7243 3 99415 2 6

Ten Years After - *Ten Years After* - Deram DML 1015

The Ventures - *Another Smash/The Ventures* - ONE 18925

The Ventures - *EP Collection* - See For Miles Records Ltd SEECD 292

The Yardbirds - *Five Live Yardbirds* - Charly CD 182

The Yardbirds - *Roger The Engineer* - Impact IMCD 9.001370

The 1970s: Maturity and Diversity

George Benson - *Breezin'* - Warner Bros WEA 256199

Larry Carlton - *Singin' Playin'* - Blue Thumb/Edsel EDCS 439

Larry Carlton - *Larry Carlton* - Blue Thumb MCA 42245

Eric Clapton - *462 Ocean* - Boulevard RSO 8116972

Eric Clapton - *E.C. Was Here* - Polydor 5318232

Larry Coryell/John McLaughlin - *Spaces* - Vanguard VMD 79345

Miles Davis - *Tribute to Jack Johnson* - Columbia 4710032

Deep Purple - *Concertos for Group and Orchestra* - EMI CZ 342

Al Di Meola - *Elegant Gypsy* - Columbia CK 34461

John McLaughlin/ Mahavishnu Orch. - *Inner Worlds* - Columbia 33908

Joe Pass - *Joe Pass, Virtuoso* - Pablo CD 2310708

Joe Pass - *Joe Pass, Portraits of Duke Ellington* - Pablo CD 2310716

Patto (Ollie Halsall) - *Patto, Sense of the Absurd* - Vertigo 528 696-2

The Police - *Regatta de Blanc* - A & M CDMID 127

Lee Ritenour - *The Captain's Journey* - Elektra K52094

Lee Ritenour - *Feel The Night* - Elektra Asylum 6E-192

Lee Ritenour - *Rit* - Elektra Musician 60196

Rolling Stones - *Exile on Main Street* - Virgin CDV 2731

Rolling Stones - *Sticky Fingers* - Virgin CDV 2730

Soft Machine (Alan Holdsworth) - *Bundles* - EMI Harvest, SHSP 4044

The Turbulent Years

Howard Alden - *Take Your Pick* - Concord CCD4732

Lenny Breau - *Lenny Breau Live at Dante's* - String Jazz SJRCD1008

Jimmy Bruno - *Live at Birdland,* Vol II - Concord CCD-4801-2

Royce Campbell/Adrian Ingram - *Hands Across The Water* - String Jazz SJRCH 1002

Albert Collins - *Ice Pickin'* - Alligator ALCD 4713

Albert Collins - *Cold Snap* - Alligator ALCD 4752

Jerry Donahue - *Neck of the Wood, Road Goes on Forever* - RGFCD011

Robben Ford - *Talk To Your Daughter* - Warner Bros 25647-1

Bill Frisell - *Bill Frisell Quartet* - Nonesuch 7559794012

Danny Gatton - *Hot Rod Guitar Anthology* - Rhino R2 75691

Danny Gatton - *In Concert 9/9/94* - Big Mo BM 2028

Alan Holdsworth - *IOU Band Live* - Outer Music CLP9970

Alan Holdsworth - *Metal Fatigue* - JM SJMS 186422

Eric Johnson - *Venus Isle* - EMI PRMCD 11

Albert Lee - *Gagged But Not Bound* - MCA MCAD 42063

Pat Martino/Various Artists - *All Sides Now* - Bleu Note 37627

Pat Metheny - *As Falls, So Falls* - Wichita Falls ECM 8214162

Nirvana - *Nevermind* - Geffen DGCD24425

Red Hot Chili Peppers - *Blood, Sugar, Sex, Magik* - Warner Bros 7599 266 812

Red Hot Chili Peppers - *Mother's Milk* - EMI 792152 2

Vernon Reid - *Mistaken Identity* - Epic 4839212

Joe Satriani - *Surfing With The Alien* - Relativity 4629732

Sonic Youth - *Daydream Nation* - Blast First BF FP34CD

Steve Vai - *Passion and Warfare* - Relativity 4671092

Eddie Van Halen - *Fair Warning* - Warner Bros WEA 9235402

Stevie Ray Vaughan - *Texas Flood* - Epic EPC 4609512

Stevie Ray Vaughan - *Couldn't Stand the Weather* - Epic EPC 4655712

Index

111

32526010R00064

Made in the USA
San Bernardino, CA
08 April 2016